Winning Grant Proposals

Winning Grant Proposals

Eleven Successful Appeals
by American Nonprofits
to Corporations, Foundations, Individuals, and
Government Agencies

Gordon Jay Frost
Editor

Fund Raising Institute, a division of
The Taft Group
12300 Twinbrook Parkway
Suite 520
Rockville, MD 20852-1607

Winning Grant Proposals

Published by
Fund Raising Institute
A Division of *The Taft Group*
12300 Twinbrook Parkway, Suite 520
Rockville, Maryland 20852

ISBN 0-930807-36-7

Fund Raising Institute publishes books on fund raising, philanthropy, and nonprofit management. To request information, or a copy of our catalog, please write us at the above address or call 1-800-877 TAFT.

The trademark ITP is used under license

Contents

Contents

The Power of Proposals

On one hand, a proposal is simply that. A case for an idea. Insubstantial. On the other, a proposal is an opportunity to give shape to an idea in the mind of the reader and to let that idea go to have a life of its own.

All successful writing relies upon a simple premise: no tears in the writer, no tears in the reader. All of the proposals in this book, whether they are for community projects or museum endowments, communicate the passion and commitment necessary to conjure up the child whose dreams are yet to be realized or the beauty and importance of the unbuilt museum.

What makes each proposal in this collection especially effective, however, is craft. And, just as a well crafted poem evokes clear images without cliche, these proposals elucidate the missions of institutions in a way that holds up under scrutiny. The arguments are as sound as the feelings behind them.

Form, style and content are the keys to their success. Each writer was aware of his or her audience and communicates in an appropriate tone. Each explains the project completely, including its benefit to the institution, the community and the benefits to the donor. At the conclusion, the reader is aware of the answers to the six basic questions which every proposal must answer: who, what, when, where, why and how. Solid research and consultation with the prospect in advance of the solicitation are two ways in which to determine exactly how those answers should be framed and what specific issues should be addressed.

The institutions which agreed to participate in this collection selected the works they wished to include by themselves. The only direction they were given was to supply a proposal of which they were especially proud, both for its quality and its success, that had received support since 1990. The result is a fairly diverse lot, with applications to corporations, foundations, individuals and the U.S. government. Request sizes are similarly varied, with grants ranging from $5,000 to $1 million. They are not grouped in any particular order. Each has something of value to those of us looking for examples of good work.

Each proposal is preceded by a brief preface introducing the institution, the proposal author(s) and providing some history of the relationship between the donor and recipient prior to the gift. Several of the proposals have cover letters included for reference and most include budgets.

Interestingly, in a decade of increased access to desktop publishing, while all the proposals looked professional, none were particularly distinctive visually. Typefaces and sizes were generally the same and everything was printed on white paper. (A notable exception: the proposal to the National Endowment for the Arts is reproduced, in part, from the original application forms.) This should come as a comfort to both those without top notch equipment or who have always believed that quality, not multiple typefaces, is what ultimately catches the donor's eye.

i

In preparing the proposals for this book, proposals were altered to conform to standard manuscript format, including justified margins and single-spacing. Typographical clues in the original manuscripts, such as headings, bold face type, budget organization, underlining and indented or otherwise highlighted areas have been retained.

Please use the proposals in this book as you would any good writing. Be inspired by them. Try to surpass them. And look to each as proof that any dream, if well articulated, has a waiting audience.

* * * * *

My personal thanks and gratitude to the many authors who contributed to this collection, each of whom is profiled in the notes preceding their respective works, and the institutions where they practice their craft. I am proud to have been able to work with each of them. Many thanks to the many others who assisted me in making contact with contributors, especially Lily Beck, Patricia Smith, Tim Ambrose, Jon Thorsen, Margaret Fuhry, Marty Walsh, Jim Morrison, Mary Lou Siebert, David Thompson, Lyn Day, Jim Yunker and the American Prospect Research Association. And, most of all, thanks to Yuko Iida Frost for allowing me to monopolize the computer and being so kind about my staying up until all hours to complete this project.

Winning Grant Proposals

Success with a European Foundation:
RIT Imaging Proposal Helps Hasselblad Get the Picture

The Institution: The Rochester Institute of Technology is the 17th largest private university in the United States, providing its 13,000 students more than 200 undergraduate and 50 graduate programs. Its signature academic programs include the National Technical Institute for the Deaf, the Center for Microelectronic Engineering, the School of American Craftsmen, and the Chester F. Carlson Center for Imaging Science.

The Author: The technical portion of this proposal was written by James M. Reilly, Director of RIT's Image Permanence Institute since 1985. Other sections were written by Carolyn E. Kourofsky, Director of Prospect Research and chief proposal writer of RIT's Office of Development.

Background: As Carolyn Kourofsky writes, "while it is unusual to approach a foundation in another country, the Erna and Victor Hasselblad Foundation seemed a natural for RIT because of its commitment to supporting research in photography. RIT is known internationally for its School of Photographic Arts & Sciences and Center for Imaging Science, which offered this country's first doctoral program in imaging science. Furthermore, its home city of Rochester, New York is the birthplace of Eastman Kodak and is known for its imaging industries.

"Initial contact with the Foundation was made in 1986 when a faculty member made a request to the Foundation and received funding for high speed electronic imaging apparatus. A larger proposal that included Mr. Reilly's request for support for the Image Permanence Institute was sent in December 1990. This was followed up in February 1991 by a visit to the Foundation by RIT's Vice-President for Development. It was only during this visit that we learned of another connection between the Foundation and the city of Rochester: Mr. Hasselblad had worked at Eastman Kodak and its founder, George Eastman, had given him some stock during Kodak's early days, which was reinvested and helped to build the Hasselblad fortune."

The Hasselblad Foundation came through with 460,000 Swedish kronas (U.S. $70,886) for the Image Permanence Institute. The proposal excerpts which follow pertain to this request.

1

PROPOSAL TO
THE ERNA AND VICTOR HASSELBLAD FOUNDATION

from
ROCHESTER INSTITUTE OF TECHNOLOGY

for support of
RESEARCH IN PHOTOGRAPHY AND IMAGING

DECEMBER 1990

[PROPOSAL] CONTENTS

ABSTRACT

Rochester Institute of Technology (RIT) is internationally known for its unique resources in the study and research of photography and imaging. It is located in Rochester, New York, U.S.A., a city which is home to Eastman Kodak Company and Xerox Corporation, and has been called the ''Imaging Capital of the World.'' RIT's reputation in graphic arts and photography provide a prestigious history and foundation for pursuing new applications in photography and imaging.

RIT offers the only doctoral program in Imaging Science in North America, and its new Center for Imaging Science is the largest academic facility devoted to imaging science on the continent. From this institution will come the imaging scientists of the future, to fuel research and development in such fields as silver halide research, electronographic cameras, photographic preservation, and color measurement.

RIT invites the Erna and Victor Hasselblad Foundation to become a significant participant in the photographic and imaging work of the Institute. We seek total support of $311,880. This includes support for the four major projects described in this proposal as well as $50,000 for RIT's College of Science, which provides subject matter support for all of the graphic arts programs.

ROCHESTER INSTITUTE OF TECHNOLOGY:
A PARTNERSHIP WITH INDUSTRY

A distinctive educational institution since 1829, Rochester Institute of Technology (RIT) is recognized throughout the United States and internationally as a resource for instruction in the latest technologies. A recent *U.S. News & World Report* survey of "America's Best Colleges" ranked RIT second in the northeast for quality of academic reputation. RIT was also selected by Peterson's *Competitive Colleges 1990-1991*, a listing of universities that consistently accept the nation's best students.

RIT is known world-wide for its excellence in emerging technologies. It initiated the nation's first undergraduate degree program in microelectronic engineering in 1982, and built the Center for Microelectronic and Computer Engineering with the input and support of the industry. The Institute is the only university in the country to offer a bachelor's, master's, and doctoral program in Imaging Science. The undergraduate computer science program is the largest in the country, and the School of Photographic Arts and Science is internationally recognized.

The 17th largest private university in the country, its partnership with industry involves educating future business executives, engineers, and other professionals to fill vital functions in today's technical world, as well as providing industry with workshops, training courses, and consulting in various fields.

Through its nine colleges -- the Colleges of Applied Science and Technology, Business, Continuing Education, Engineering, Fine and Applied Arts, Graphic Arts and Photography, Liberal Arts, and Science, and the National Technical Institute for the Deaf -- RIT educates its 13,000 students in more than 200 undergraduate and 50 graduate programs. The placement rate of RIT graduates attests to its success: over 90 percent of RIT alumni secure employment in their career fields within one year of graduation.

RIT was one of the first educational institutions in the country to offer cooperative work experience, initiating its program in 1912. Today the co-op program is the fourth oldest and fifth largest in the world, providing both work experience and financial resources for students. More than 1,300 companies and 2,700 students participate in over 4,000 co-op placements. Many of these employers hire graduating co-op students.

RIT is proud of its record in providing quality education to all who seek it. Thirty-five percent of RIT's full-time undergraduates are the first in their families to attend college. Women make up 40 percent of RIT's student body, up from 15 percent fifteen years ago. To deal with the singular needs of minority students, RIT established an Office of Minority Affairs in 1982.

RIT attracts students from all 50 states and more than 60 foreign countries. Such diversity reflects the wide-range appeal and reputation of the Institute, which has the highest record of incoming transfer students among four-year colleges/ universities in New York State. There are more than 60,000 RIT alumni throughout the world.

THE SCHOOL OF PHOTOGRAPHIC ARTS AND SCIENCES

Graduates of RIT's School of Photographic Arts and Sciences (SPAS) are well known in the photographic field. The school is proud of the five Pulitzer Prizes won by its graduates, all within the past thirteen years.

The school was founded in 1930 at the request of industrial photographic interests. These included Bausch and Lomb Optical Company, Defender Photo Supply Company (now the E.I. duPont de Nemours Company), Haloid Company (now the Xerox Corporation), and the Eastman Kodak Company. The educational objective was to provide trained employees for such organizations.

The evolution of SPAS since that time has included the introduction of a B.S. and then an M.S. in Photographic Science in 1955 and 1965, the addition of the Imaging and Photographic Science program and the Center for Imaging Science in 1985, the construction of a new 75,000-square foot facility to house the Center, and the establishment of a Ph.D. program for Imaging Science beginning in September 1990.

Today the School for Photographic Arts and Sciences is comprised of eight departments. These are designed for careers in the following areas:

Applied Photography -- advertising, editorial/magazine photography, and
　　photojournalism
Biomedical Photographic Communications -- photographic work in hospitals,
　　medical research centers and other health institutions
Film and Video -- moving image through film, video and animation
Fine Arts Photography -- combining art and photography
Imaging and Photographic Technology -- scientific and technical photography,
　　including areas such as technical and sales representatives, photographic
　　instrumentation, and product development and testing.
Photographic Processing and Finishing Management -- laboratory supervision
　　and management positions in the photographic processing and finishing
　　industry.
Image Permanence -- film restoration and preservation.

WINNING GRANT PROPOSALS

The School of Photographic Arts and Sciences has 47 full-time faculty members serving the needs of over 800 undergraduate and graduate students. The facility offers 190 darkrooms, 50 studios and nine specialized laboratories. A complete selection of photographic equipment is available for loan to students.

THE CENTER FOR IMAGING SCIENCE

The Chester F. Carlson Center for Imaging Science at RIT offers graduate and undergraduate degree programs and is involved in research and development activities for industry and government. Established in 1985, it has been designated by the trustees of Rochester Institute of Technology as an RIT Center of Excellence. It is a unique national and international resource.

The Center includes fifteen full-time faculty, eight interdisciplinary graduate faculty assigned to the Ph.D. program, and over 100 undergraduate and 80 M.S. students. When fully operational, the Ph.D. program will enroll between 25 and 40 students. Areas of teaching and research interest include:

o Digital Image Processing
o Remote Sensing
o Image Evaluation
o Electronic Printing
o Holography
o Optical Design
o Machine Vision
o Microlithography

o Color Science
o Electrophotography
o Solid State Imaging
o Image Perception
o Medical Diagnostic Imaging
o Chemical Imaging Processes
o Electro-Optical Instrumentation

Corporate Founders and Industrial Associates of the Center include Eastman Kodak Company, Xerox Corporation, IBM, Dainippon Ink and Chemicals, E.I. duPont de Nemours & Company, Fuji Photo Film Company, Hewlett-Packard, Toppan Printing Company and Polaroid.

IMAGING SCIENCE--A DISCIPLINE OF THE FUTURE

In this century the formal study of conventional silver halide materials and camera systems has matured to the extent that courses in photographic science are relatively commonplace.

In recent years, the number of new imaging technologies, devices and recording processes has multiplied. Electrophotography, microlithography, CCD arrays, laser writers, and ink-jet printers are just a few examples of these new processes and technologies. Similarly, image processing, color reproduction, image analysis and perception of images have emerged as disciplines of quite general interest, and not solely from the viewpoint of how they relate to the field of silver halide photography.

At the same time, the fields of practical application have broadened in range. Remote sensing, digital graphics, diagnostic imaging, image transmission, storage and retrieval are examples of fields that require a generalized understanding of principles and techniques well beyond those of camera and film.

The need to extend established and traditional university studies and research in photographic science and optics into these newer and emerging fields has led to the recent evolution of more comprehensive courses and research. In spite of the diverse technologies and applications, many underlying principles are the same because the task of converting an object into an image is the common theme. These common fundamental principles have been collected under the heading of imaging science.

IMAGE PERMANENCE INSTITUTE

Co-sponsored by RIT and the Society for Imaging Science and Technology, the Image Permanence Institute (IPI) was formed as a neutral and independent scientific laboratory. It is the world's largest independent laboratory devoted to research in photographic preservation. IPI enjoys an international reputation for its work with microfilm preservation, archival storage enclosures research, and especially film base preservation research.

Research

IPI performs contract work for organizations and institutions and also research work resulting from grants. The staff scientists are active in leadership roles on photographic permanence standards in the American National Standards Institute and the International Standards Organization. Consulting in the area of image stability is also becoming an important aspect of its services.

IPI is currently completing two large research projects. The first began as a project to study selenium toning of microfilm, to determine whether toning has any effect on microfilm's stability. Further funding is needed to continue this project, but using sulfiding instead of selenium for the toning. Questions to be explored include whether sulfiding protection extends to other pollutants; whether protection is short-lived or long-lasting, how to treat microfilm for maximum through-put on automated processor equipment; whether protection is effective for pictorial films and papers;

and whether there is any adverse effect on information content, image quality or emulsion physical properties in microfilm.

The second project is basic scientific research into the deterioration of cellulose acetate films (safety film). It will provide archives with a knowledge of the practical storage recommendations to ensure preservation of existing safety film in collections.

A large study was recently undertaken to determine the effect of pollutant gases on microfilm. Two chambers have been custom made to allow film to be exposed to known, controlled amounts of nitrogen dioxide, ozone, sulfur dioxide and hydrogen sulfide under controlled temperature and humidity conditions.

Staff

Five scientists, with experience in the preservation and stability of photographic prints and films, staff the Image Permanence Institute. The back-up staff is augmented by several graduate students who are doing further training in photographic conservation. Unpaid interns are accepted to work in exchange for the opportunity for learning and use of the IPI library and other resources.

Facilities

Equipment in IPI includes a series of temperature-humidity controlled ovens that are suitable for incubation and accelerated aging studies. Density measurements can be made on both black and white and color materials, both in the reflection and transmission mode. Facilities are available to feed densitometer readings into a computer for storage or for further analysis and calculation.

Physical testing equipment can measure tensile properties, curl, brittleness, dimensional stability, abrasion and blocking. These physical measurements are made at a controlled temperature and relative humidity. Equipment has been set up to evaluate the light fading characteristics of photographic images. This includes a high intensity xenon arc and in the future, will include low intensity fluorescent bulbs. The chemical laboratory can do measurements for residual hypo testing and the photographic activity test. (Testing of photographic enclosures to ensure that they are safe for the storage of photographs.)

IPI has a strong expertise in the identification of 19th century print material. Means of identification of such prints are described in a recent book by Professor James M. Reilly. For educational purposes, a large collection of 19th century prints represent the many processes that were available. IPI also houses a large collection of prints displaying defects and degradation that photographs of all types can experience. This collection is of great value in the training of film conservation.

Needs

RIT seeks $86,680 U.S. (466,272 SEK) from the Hasselblad Foundation to purchase a walk-in environmental chamber for use in the Image Permanence Institute's ongoing program of research in cinema and sheet film preservation. The equipment is needed to pre-condition film samples in a large research project concerning the value of low RH in extending the life of cinema and still films. The project has received support from the U.S. National Endowment for the Humanities, but that grant did not include funds for necessary equipment.

HASSELBLAD FOUNDATION

TOTAL PROPOSED GRANT BUDGET

EQUIPMENT
Silver Halide Laboratory

Evaporator	$10,000	
Turbo pump	$10,000	
Staff computers	$9,000	
Emulsion lab	$12,000	
Absorptance spectrometer	$20,000	
Upgrade sensitometer	$10,000	
Construct new sensitometer	$7,000	
Upgrade parallel processor	$40,000	
		$118,000 (625,400 SEK)

SPAS Imaging Department	
Operation of a MarkII EG Camera	$38,200 (202,460 SEK)
Spectrometer CM-100	$19,000 (100,700 SEK)
Image Permanence Laboratory	
Walk-in environmental chamber	$86,680 (459,404 SEK)
Optical Laboratory	$75,826 (401,877 SEK)
TOTAL EQUIPMENT BUDGET	$337,706 (1,789,841 SEK)
COLLEGE OF SCIENCE SUPPORT	$50,000 (265,000 SEK)
TOTAL REQUEST	$387,706 (2,054,841 SEK)

Success with Seminars:
Women Judges' Fund Makes a Good Case to Noyes Foundation

The Institution: In 1979 the National Association of Women Judges (NAWJ) was founded by women judges dedicated to strengthening the role of women in the American judicial system. NAWJ has grown rapidly since its founding and now has over 1,000 members, including men and women judges from all 50 states. In 1980 the Board of Directors and the members of NAWJ founded The Foundation for Women Judges, now called the Women Judges' Fund for Justice (WJFJ), as an independent non-profit educational and research organization designed to focus on issues and concerns of NAWJ's members and of the American legal and judicial system. WJFJ's mission is to improve the administration of justice, particularly with issues that impact on women in the justice system. WJFJ has been particularly effective in developing model programs focused on cutting edge issues such as: bioethics, biotechnology and the law; gender bias in the court systems; and accessing the judicial selection process.

The Author: This proposal was written by Eugene A. Scanlan, Ph.D., CFRE, Senior Consultant and Manager, Eastern Regional Office, Alford, Ver Schave & Associates, Inc. Mr. Scanlan has been involved with not-fot-profits for over twenty-six years. His experience includes serving as a professional staff member of one of the largest foundations in the country; he has also held management, contuling, development, and teaching positions with organizations including national, regional, and local groups, colleges and universities. He has published several general and specific articles on non-profit management and fund raising. He is President-Elect of the Greater Washington D.C. Area Chapter of the National Society of Fund Raising Executives.

Background: Mr. Scanlan and Marilyn Nejelski, Executive Director of WJFJ, visited the foundation, a prior donor, to discuss some new programs. The Noyes Foundation staff member suggested a new idea: put together a program to replicate the WJFJ educational workshops nationally through the state judicial education programs. Ms. Nejelski talked to WJFJ's program committee about the idea and they were enthusiastic about the concept. The Noyes Foundation staff suggested the grant size and a proposal was written in accordance with their discussions. As a result of the grant, the WJFJ makes mini-grants to provide the WJFJ programs on a state basis, thereby reaching larger audiences.

July 12, 1992

Jael Silliman, Program Officer
The Jessie Smith Noyes Foundation
16 East 34th Street
New York, NY 10016

Dear Jael:

Thank you again for meeting with me in February and for taking the time to speak with me in June about the concept paper the Women Judges' Fund for Justice (WJFJ) submitted to The Jessie Smith Noyes Foundatlon. We are most appreciative of the past support from the Noyes Foundation for the Fund's continuing work in bioethics and also appreciate the opportunity to submit another proposal focused on this area.

We are requesting consideration by the Noyes Foundation of a grant of $30,000 to the Women Judges' Fund for Justice to support our educational programs on bioethics and the law at the state level.

In our meeting with you and in our concept paper we presented an outline for the establishment by the Women Judges' Fund for Justice of a small fund to help insure states could set up their own judicial education programs based upon those developed by the Fund. As you know, WJFJ continually seeks to create model programs in areas such as bioethics and the law; gender bias in the courts with regard to child custody and visitation, spousal support, reproductive responsibilities and family violence; and a program on pregnant substance abusers developed for the American Bar Association meeting on August 9. The program on pregnant substance abusers will also be presented to judges in Washington state on August 24 . Enclosed is a copy of the information on this important program.

Currently WJFJ cannot provide the support and staff necessary to replicate these programs at the state level through existing state judicial education programs. WJFJ can only provide interested states wlth our materials, suggest possible speakers, and give the benefit of our experience along with some encouragement. The states themselves, due to increasingly severe budget constraints, are frequently not able to develop programs of their own nor support the presentation of new programs such as those WJFJ develops. However, a small amount of money, usually only a few thousand dollars, will provide the necessary seed funds to enable states to replicate our programs. In most cases a relatively small amount of money determines whether or not a state can have a bioethics and the law seminar for its judges.

We are therefore proposing that The Jessie Smith Noyes Foundation consider a one year grant of $30,000 to the Women Judges' Fund for Justice. Of this amount,

$25,000 would be placed in a special account to provide support funds to states wishing to replicate our current and planned bioethics and the law programs.

To encourage the replication of our programs as widely as possible and maximize the use of the funds, no one state would be eligible to receive support totaling more than $5,000 within one year from the inception of the program. In order to insure high quality programs we will develop an application, review, and reporting/evaluation process, with a special committee of our Board of Directors established to oversee the program. We are also considering having other individuals involved in the review process. We will try to keep the process fairly simple but want to insure adequate review and oversight of the program. The remaining $5,000 of the $30,000 requested would be used to partially support the administrative costs of the program.

You will note that this is a change from our original concept paper in that we have decided not to pursue the addition of another WJFJ staff member to oversee the program.

I have enclosed our detailed proposal and supporting information. In the proposal I have sought to address the specific questions you raised in our phone conversation as well as cover the key points in the Foundation's outline. If you do need more information, please call me. Thank you and we look forward to The Jessie Smith Noyes Foundation's consideration of this proposal.

Sincerely,

Marilyn Nejelski
Executive Director

Bioethics and the Law:

A proposal to enable state judicial educators to carry out education and training programs on bioethics and the law designed by the Women Judges' Fund for Justice

Grant Request:
$30,000

Purposes:
Project Costs $25,000
Administrative $5,000

Submitted By:
Women Judges' Fund for Justice
733 15th Street, N.W.
Suite 700
Washington, DC 20005

Contact Person:
Marilyn Nejelski
Executive Director
(202) 783-2073

Date:
July 14, 1992

Women Judges' Fund for Justice
The Organization

History

In 1979 the National Association of Women Judges (NAWJ) was founded by women judges dedicated to strengthening the role of women in the American judicial system. NAWJ has grown rapidly since its founding and now has nearly 1,200 members, including men and women judges from all 50 states. In 1980 the Board of Directors and the members of NAWJ established The Foundation for Women Judges, now called the Women Judges' Fund for Justice (WJFJ), as an independent non-profit educational and research organization designed to focus on issues and concerns of NAWJ's members and of the American legal and judicial system.

Mission

WJFJ's mission is to improve the administration of justice, particularly with issues that impact on women in the justice system. WJFJ has been effective in developing model programs focused on cutting edge issues such as: bioethics, biotechnology and the law, gender bias in the court systems, and accessing the judicial selection process. Many of WJFJ's programs are designed to become part of ongoing programs, such as state judicial education programs, the National Judicial College curriculum, etc.

Governance and Staff

The Women Judges' Fund for Justice is overseen by a 15 member Board of Directors. The Board is organized into several committees which meet regularly to set goals, review progress, and deal with other aspects of the Fund activities. The major standing committees are the Executive Committee, the Project Development Committee, the Finance Committee, the Resource Development Committee and Personnel Committee.

The staff of the Fund maintains offices in Washington, D.C. and includes the Executive Director and an Executive Assistant. From time to time interns have been employed to assist with particular projects of the Fund. While the staff is small, the ongoing work of the Fund is supplemented by extensive volunteer involvement of many of the members of NAWJ who serve on the standing and special committees as well as provide advice and assistance on an individual basis. Additionally, the Fund retains project managers or consultants from time to time to supplement staff work as well as to provide the needed expertise. For example, a legal expert on bioethics was hired as a consultant to develop the five highly successful bioethics conferences and the Fund has employed a consultant to work on the Pregnant Substance Abusers Project.

Budget and Income Sources

The Fund's 1992 operating budget is $235,840. Primary support for ongoing operating costs of the Fund include a portion of dues from NAWJ members (6% of FY 1991 income), a direct allocation from the NAWJ budget each year (2% of FY 1991 income), and individual contributions from NAWJ members (8% of FY 1991 income), other fund raising activities (12% of FY 1991 income), and operating grants (4% of FY 1991 income). Grants and gifts for projects and programs of the Fund as well as the above income sources provided the Fund with a total of $329,962 in FY 1991.

Fund Raising

Fund raising focuses on three areas: support of projects and programs (primarily from foundations and other grant-making organizations), support of general operating costs (primarily from NAWJ and its members, operating grants, and administrative overhead on project grants), and development of longer-term general support from new sources including those who identify with the mission and goals of the Fund. Several years ago the Fund retained counsel to assess the organization and to make specific recommendations in the areas of governance, planning and fund raising. A central recommendation of the report was the need for the Fund to develop non-foundation ongoing sources of support to meet its basic operating expenses. The report recommended the establishment of a National Advisory Committee to take on the responsibility of raising funds for operating support (in part, because judges are generally prohibited from engaging in fund raising activities). A 12 member National Advisory Committee is now in place and has undertaken the task of meeting the operating expenses of the Fund.

Over the long term, primary sources of support for the Fund are seen as:

A portion of NAWJ members' dues, a yearly contribution from NAWJ, and individual contributions from NAWJ members (in response to two appeals per year), all to be used towards operating expenses;

National Advisory Committee fund raising, with sources to include contributions by members of the Committee and/or their firms or businesses, as well as contributions from other companies, law firms, and individuals concerned about the issues being addressed by the Fund. These funds will also primarily be used to meet operating costs; and

Corporate and private foundations and quasi-public agencies (such as the State Justice Institute) for support of projects and programs of the Fund. For reasons of cost efficiency and planning, projects are generally grouped into programs which last a period of 2 - 3 years (such as the Bioethics and the Law Program), after which they are evaluated and, if appropriate, a new series of projects is created.

Efforts are continually made to seek new sources of support for the Fund. Over the last few years eleven new sources have been successfully approached for support of the work of the Fund. Because of the unique emphasis of the Fund on education of judges on issues affecting women and children, the Fund must continually show potential supporters both of the need to educate judges and the success record of WJFJ in meeting this need. While millions of dollars are granted for service programs, policy research and development, public education, legal action and legislative activity, almost no money is granted for working with the third branch of government - the judicial sector. Yet judges' decisions often directly affect not only individuals but society at large. An informed and educated judiciary, like an informed and educated electorate, is necessary for the survival of democracy. It has been suggested that a more constructive way to handle bioethics cases is through litigation. However, even from a simple cost efficiency standpoint, it is more effective to bring together 50 to 100 judges to be presented with background information on issues such as bioethics and to discuss current law and possible future directions the law will take than it is to carry out litigation over a 2-3 year period.

Activities and Accomplishments

The Women Judges' Fund for Justice has focused its primary activities on the following areas over the past several years:

Bioethics and the Law: Programs and projects have included workshops, seminars, and the recent future-directed National Conference on Bioethics, Family and the Law. All were designed to provide an intensive introduction and updating on the current state of the law on these issues, the impact of technology on the law, bioethical thinking, and possible decision-making processes. The overall objective in each case was to provide judges with both background knowledge and a framework for informed decisionmaking. Over the past several years, well over 300 judges have attended these programs, which have been highly rated by participants. (See enclosure for an information sheet and agenda.)

Medicine, Ethics, and the Law: Pre-Conception to Birth: This program is designed to provide information to state court judges about the medical, legal, and ethical issues that arise at the beginning of life. It addresses the topics of forced contraception, assisted reproduction (artificial insemination, in vitro fertilization, surrogate parenting), drug abusing pregnant women, medical decisions during pregnancy, forced cesarean sections, and the treatment of extremely premature infants. The goal of the course is to aid judges in developing a coherent and cohesive judicial approach to deciding cases that involve these issues. (See enclosure for an agenda and biographical information on faculty.)

Gender Bias and the Courts: This ongoing program of the Fund reflects the concerns of its founders of the need to both document gender bias in the court systems of the country (as it affects both participants in the judicial system and judicial decisionmaking) and to develop specific recommendations for solutions to gender-bias related problems. Long before sexual harassment became a topic of public interest, the Fund was working through the state gender bias task forces, usually established under the aegis of the chief justices of the state supreme courts, to document the problem. The Fund is currently working with the National Center for State Courts in organizing the "Second National Conference on Gender Bias in the Courts: Focus on Followup." This conference is planned for March of 1993 and will bring together representatives from the 35 states that have established gender bias task forces, members of the federal judiciary, and individuals from states which do not at present have gender bias task forces. The overall goals are to assist the task forces that have written reports with implementation of their findings, to assist those task forces that are in the early stages of development with the gathering of information and writing of their reports, and to encourage those states without gender bias task forces to establish them.

"You Be The Judge" series: These programs are targeted primarily to women lawyers and are designed to be state specific (in many states judges are elected, in other states judges are appointed, and in some states there are both elected and appointed judges). The seminars acquaint those interested in becoming judges with both the process to be followed and the key individuals who are part of that process. To date, seven states have conducted ''You Be The Judge'' seminars and WJFJ estimates that nearly 500 individuals have participated in these sessions. The program was so successful that California has held two seminars and Maryland has held three. A substantial number of seminar participants have gone on to become judges.

Special projects: The Fund has undertaken a number of special projects based upon both needs and the interests of the leadership of the Fund. These include projects focused on family violence, child custody and visitation and spousal support in divorce proceedings, reproductive responsibilities, substance abuse by pregnant women, and a planned demonstration project in California to better integrate the court and social service delivery systems for families at risk.

The Proposal

Background and Justification

The Women Judges' Fund for Justice has had a national impact beyond its staff size and budget. Over the last 13 years the Fund has developed programs which have subsequently been adopted by other judicial education programs at the national and state levels. Thus a major emerging role for the Fund is to design, create and test programs which can be used by other judicial educators in their own settings.

To a large extent, the Fund's programs continue to be successful and well-received because they are designed to provide information and stimulate debate while keeping a sense of balance in the information, concepts and opinions expressed. Thus judges have come to see that they will not be presented with only one side or a single point of view but will rather receive well balanced background information. One result of this approach has frequently been capacity attendance at Fund programs.

The Women Judges' Fund for Justice is now one of the leading national organizations developing judicial education programs concerned with judicial-related issues affecting women and children. Its work in the area of bioethics has been particularly strong. One recent example of its impact is the Fund's planned special panel presentation, "What's a Judge to Do? Pregnant Substance Users and the Role of the Courts." This program will be presented at the 1992 American Bar Association Annual Meeting on August 10, 1992. The program is funded in part by the Henry J. Kaiser Family Foundation and the National Judicial College and will educate the bar and the bench on this important topic. The program will cover:

The medical basis of chemical dependency and its effect on the unborn child;

How judicial responses to perinatal drug and alcohol exposure differ depending on the socio-economic status and race of the mother; and

The exercise of discretion in criminal and family cases.

The panel will focus on these and other issues and will explore possible guidelines for alternative approaches to the issues. Additional background information and newly-developed materials will be available to participants.

This presentation and the Medicine, Law and Ethics program are examples of issues of growing concern to the Women Judges' Fund for Justice. In the past WJFJ educational programs have been used by organizations ranging from the National Judicial College to state and local judicial education programs. The Fund has found that one of the most effective means of insuring its judicial education programs reach a wider audience is through state judicial education systems. Each state has in some way organized judicial education to insure there is an ongoing opportunity for judges to receive additional information and training in relevant areas. Some states have formal programs, with full-time staff assigned to this function, while others have a less formal approach. In many states judges are required to participate in continuing education programs. Thus the best outlet for replication of Fund programs on a broader scale is the state judicial education programs. Given the Fund's limited resources, it falls to these programs to insure that the Fund's work, once tested and proven, will reach a broader audience of judges. For example, the program on pregnant substance abusers cited above has already been requested for replication in the State of Washington and will be presented there on August 24.

However, states and state judicial education programs are facing increasingly-difficult budgetary situations with little or no funding for new programs such as those developed by the Fund. Thus emerging critical issues for the judiciary are frequently not addressed by parallel judicial education programs.

The Women Judges' Fund for Justice sees in this situation an unusual opportunity to both continue its work to develop meaningful judicial education programs and to serve as a catalyst to insure broader utilization of these programs at the state level. In many cases the Fund's programs, if utilized by states, will be the only judicial education opportunities available on the issues being addressed by WJFJ.

The Proposed Plan

After careful examination of many factors, including participants' evaluations of past Fund programs, responses from state judicial educators, and continuing interest expressed in replication of Fund bioethics and the law programs, the Women Judges' Fund for Justice is proposing to develop a pilot project to enable state judicial education systems to use its current and future seminars. This plan, while requiring minimal financial and staff resources to implement it, would enable a wider utilization of the resources of the Fund while insuring more judges are reached throughout the country.

As envisioned by the Fund and presented in our concept paper to the Jessie Smith Noyes Foundation, the specific steps for this one-year pilot project are:

> Obtaining of $25,000 in funds;

> Establishment of a special fund at WJFJ to provide seed money for state judicial education programs wishing to replicate current and planned bioethics and the law judicial education programs of the Fund;
> Creating a special oversight committee to develop guidelines and the application process, review requests for support, and develop specific evaluation criteria;

> Limiting the maximum amount to any one state to $5,000 during the one year test of the concept;

> Informing state judicial educators and the chief judicial official of each state (usually the chief justice of the state supreme court) of the availability of the funds and the application process;

> Processing applications in accordance with the guidelines and procedures, and awarding grants of seed money; and

> Evaluating the effectiveness of the pilot program in creating wider adoption of WJFJ educational seminars and workshops.

The overall goal of the planned program will be to insure that Women Judges' Fund for Justice bioethics and the law programs, such as the pregnant substance abuse panel, are available to the widest possible audience of judges after each program is developed and tested by the Fund. Even a minimal investment of funds will help insure more states can use these programs in their judicial education system.

Funding provided to the states' judicial education programs would only be utilized for the direct costs related to replication of WJFJ bioethics and the law programs at the state level. Funds would not replace existing state funds available for this purpose but only would supplement these funds. The review and approval process would require a clear demonstration of need on the part of applying state judicial education programs.

One question that might be raised is: "Why should a small nonprofit agency provide funds for judicial education that should be provided through the states themselves?" Our experience is that states are generally already financially restricted and judicial education programs, especially new programs related to women's issues, are not well supported. Such programs may be seen as an "add on" to the existing judicial education curricula rather than an essential part of the curricula. The strong positive response to our programs to date shows a high level of interest in the subject matter and the balanced approach we take. We believe that making these programs even more available will help additional judges develop new ways of thinking about the issues and hopefully result in more balanced and sensitive judicial decisions.

An additional benefit of the program will be the development of even stronger ties between the state judicial educators and the Women Judges' Fund for Justice. Currently, relationships between state judicial educators and the Fund exist because of the individual interest of the educators in the programs of the Fund. The establishment of a funding mechanism will help build stronger and more formal ties between the Fund and judicial education systems in the states.

Timetable

Upon receipt of the funds, WJFJ would implement the following projected one-year timetable for this project:

First Six Weeks

Formation of oversight committee for the project and first meeting held; the meeting will focus on establishing guidelines and the application process and also developing the announcement of the program which will be sent to all state judicial educators and the chief justice of each state's supreme court.

Mailing by WJFJ of announcements and application materials.

Second Six Weeks

Receipt of completed applications and beginning of processing and review by committee.

Notification to awardees and beginning of schedule coordination for programs.

25

Next 9 Months

Implementation of bioethics and the law judicial education programs.

Evaluation of results and impact of the pilot funding program by the committee.

Completion of a final report on the project and recommendations for next steps.

Evaluation

Evaluation of the pilot funding program will focus on one central issue: how many state judicial education programs that otherwise would not have been able to do so were able to replicate WJFJ bioethics and the law seminars? Also included in the process, as with all WJFJ programs, will be participant evaluation of each of the programs that are presented. The oversight committee will be responsible for developing the specific evaluation criteria and staff of the Fund will be responsible for carrying out the evaluation process, probably through a simple questionnaire sent to both judicial educators receiving funding and those applying but not receiving funding.

Expected Results

As stated earlier, it is expected that the provision of small amounts of funds to state judicial education programs for replication of WJFJ bioethics and the law seminars will enable the Fund to effectively reach a much larger audience of judges than otherwise will be possible. Thus many more judges will receive information and viewpoints on issues of concern to women and will hopefully revise their frameworks for judicial decision making. An additional outcome of this program will be the introduction to state judicial education systems of new curricular areas and new approaches for presenting critical information, as well as a broader range of presenters. For example, WJFJ programs on bioethics and the law bring together as faculty judges, medical doctors (including pediatricians and gynecologists), ethicists, legal experts, social workers, philosophers and others who present a detailed explanation of their respective decision-making processes for real cases.

Administrative and Planning Costs

In addition to the $25,000 requested for implementation of WJFJ seminars by the state judicial education programs, the Women Judges' Fund for Justice is seeking an additional $5,000 towards the administrative costs and related expenses of managing this program, including staff time, printing and mailings, and costs for the first steering committee meeting, etc.

Future Activities and Support

This program is designed to be a demonstration project of the impact of a small amount of supplemental funding on state judicial education on women's issues. It is also designed to begin to insure that women's issues are addressed in state judicial education programs. Longer term, the Fund envisions development of several easily-duplicated educational programs on key issues in such areas as bioethics and the law and making these available to state judicial education programs. It is anticipated that the pilot project will help create a greater demand for such programs and will also enable state judicial educators to re-order their priorities to include more women's issue-oriented seminars and workshops. Support for WJFJ's continuing work in this area will, of necessity, be sought from a variety of sources including foundations, corporations, individuals, law firms, etc., as well as from organizations such as the State Justice Institute. It is also anticipated that increased levels of general operating support will enable the Fund to have greater flexibility in generating new and improved programs.

Grant Request

The Women Judges' Fund for Justice requests a one-year grant of $30,000 from the Jessie Smith Noyes Foundation to be used as follows:

$25,000 to help provide partial support for state judicial education programs wishing to replicate WJFJ seminars on bioethics and the law;

$5,000 to cover administrative and oversight committee expenses associated with this program.

27

Women Judges' Fund for Justice

Program to Provide Partial Support for Implementation of Fund Bioethics and the Law Seminars by State Judicial Education Systems

Budget

Funds for Partial Support of Program Implementation	$25,000
Administrative costs associated with program	
Executive Director (3% of time)	$1,400
Executive Assistant (5% of time)	$1,050
One meeting of Oversight Committee	$1,900
Duplication, printing and mailings	$550
Miscellaneous, telephone, etc.	$100
Total	$30,000

Success with Celluloid:
Vassar Treatment of Film Education Gets Positive Review

The Institution: Vassar College was founded in 1861 in Poughkeepsie, New York as a liberal arts college for women. Vassar became coeducational in 1969 and remains committed to providing a rigorous intellectual environment conducive to liberal learning for both men and women. The Vassar student body consists of 2,200 individuals (55% women and 45% men) with approximately 22% from minority backgrounds and another 10% from foreign countries. Vassar's curriculum offers multidisciplinary and interdepartmental programs in addition to the traditional disciplines and emphasizes close faculty-student relations and collaborative faculty-student research.

The Author: Kenneth Cool is Director of Academic Program Support for Vassar College and is responsible for institutional grant programs and defining institutional priorities for the upcoming capital campaign. Dr. Cool earned his undergraduate degree from Davidson College and obtained his Masters and Doctoral degrees from Duke University, specializing in French. He previously served as Acting Director of Sponsored Projects for Santa Clara University. Also an adjunct lecturer at Vassar, he has published frequently on French literature.

Background: The development of Vassar College's proposal for an innovative aproach to the study of film, literacy and culture emerged from nearly two years of oral and written exchanges with the Henry Luce Foundation about appropriate intellectural concepts for a program grant consonant with the established philanthropic guidelines of the Luce Foundation. The basic concept for the proposal also underwent several revisions by an internal Vassar study group composed of faculty members and academic administrators. During that two-year period, the president, the dean of the faculty, and the grants officer had several telephone exchanges and face-to-face meetings with the Luce Foundation program officer.

A LUCE PROGRAM IN CINEMA, LITERACY AND CULTURE

VASSAR COLLEGE

October 23, 1989

ABSTRACT

Vassar College proposes to establish a three-year Luce Program in Cinema, Literacy and Culture that brings distinguished visiting scholars to the campus for the purpose of building a rigorous, interdisciplinary program of study focussing on new forms of visual communication and their impact on cultural literacy. The central objective of the Luce Program will be to investigate the increasing prominence of the various technological manifestations of the moving image and their effects upon the long-dormant print culture of western civilization. A related concern will focus on how the academy can incorporate these new forms of literacy into its traditional emphasis on reading and writing as the hallmark of a liberal education.

In an age when film, television and video rival the book and the newspaper as agents of information and transmitters of cultural values, it is incumbent upon colleges to teach students how to ''read'' visual documents, just as professors traditionally have taught students how to analyze novels, newspapers, political pamphlets and other linguistic manifestations of our writing-based society. Cultural sophistication and civic responsibility in the twenty-first century will require that people learn to discriminate visually with the same critical acumen that they have approached rhetoric in the past .

The Luce Program will bridge investigations of both iconic and linguistic forms of expression across a range of humanities and social science disciplines. It is important for this work that many disciplines are represented and that the study of visual expression is not relegated to a narrowly defined specialization in film. Just as writing and reading have been the shared responsibility of all disciplines, we are persuaded that the intellectual terrain of visual communication must be equally broad and encompass the methods and perspectives of literary critics, film specialists, psychologists, art historians, sociologists and philosophers -- to name a few disciplinary representatives. All have a part to play in appreciating, analyzing and teaching students how moving images open our minds to new ways of seeing the world and of expressing our relationship to it.

In practical terms, we propose to bring three distinguished scholars to the Vassar campus to enrich investigations into three aspects of visual literacy: film as theory, film as production, and film as document. The presence of these visiting scholars will help us come to grips with film as both a process of communicating and the end product of that communication. Each Luce Professor will become the standard-bearer for a number of faculty development and curricular renewal initiatives relating to his or her area of expertise .

For example, the Luce Professors will be asked to lead an annual faculty seminar that focuses on the critical vocabulary required to approach the analysis of moving images either as an aesthetic concern (film as theory), as a means of expression (film as production), or as a mode of representation (film as document).

One special dimension of the faculty seminars will be an intensive film production workshop at the end of the second year on the techniques of the medium (e.g., camera positioning, lighting strategies, editing techniques, sound mixing and screen writing).

On another level, the Luce Professors will be catalysts for new courses that approach the subject of visual literacy in provocative, interdisciplinary ways. Through the existing structure of Vassar's College Course Program, we propose to develop one introductory course that studies the concept of the visual image from historical, philosophical and psychological perspectives. Another course will take a comparative approach to narrative through various media of expression, such as the written epic, the oral folktale and the feature film. The Luce Professors will also be asked to teach one course in their area of expertise.

In addition, the Luce Professors will host an annual film program and accompanying lecture series that will serve as a broader, public forum for exploring one or more themes related to the central concerns of the Luce Program in Cinema, Literacy and Culture.

Contemporary culture is in the throes of a new form of literacy: the primacy of the written word is being eroded by the potency of visual images. The evidence, it seems, is everywhere: in the advertising and marketing of such disparate phenomena as consumer products, political campaigns and religious institutions. Especially compelling and perhaps revolutionary in their consequences are the visual images which seem to displace or at least reinforce forms of discourse traditionally anchored in oral communication. Young musicians now ''videotape'' their musical performances so that their fans not only ''listen'' to the lyrics but also ''see'' the visual manifestation of their message. The latest development in telephone technology makes it possible not only to ''hear'' the disembodied voice of a friend or business associate several thousand miles away but actually to ''scan'' the face of one's interlocutor on a built-in monitor. It is as if the visual image validates reality in our contemporary consciousness in ways that the written or spoken word alone can no longer satisfy.

This power and pervasiveness of iconic forms of expression are inseparable from the technological advances of our age. In another era, Gutenberg's invention of the press ushered in the print culture of pamphlets, newspapers and novels. In more recent times, the motion picture camera, the video recorder, computer graphic systems and laser beams have accounted for the rise of a number of visual genres, including movies, television programs, video performances and intermedia events. These technical accomplishments have now made it possible to record, manipulate and project images in provocative ways and, in the process, they have made the moving image an object of public fascination and a vehicle of cultural transmission.

To a very large degree, cinema represents for the twentieth century what the serial novel was to the previous two centuries. A new technology has created a new art form, and the medium has become a device for understanding our world and for seeing our relationship to it. The phrase, ''just like in the movies,'' is a frequent heuristic device for our time, just as nineteenth-century people projected their life events through the activity of reading. Flaubert's heroine, Emma Bovary, discovered her own discontent with life in the French provinces through the reading of sentimental novels; Woody Allen's protagonists displace their anguished relation to contemporary American culture through the viewing of old films. Art and experience are not easily separated from the culture and the technology in which they take shape.

At the heart of Vassar's proposal for a Luce Program in Cinema, Literacy and Culture is the question of how the academy should deal with film and its successor technologies (television, video and computer graphics), which have become the most pervasive vehicles for cultural expression in our age. It is our premise that colleges should be able to teach students to ''read'' films in interdisciplinary ways, just as professors from a range of disciplines have taught them how to read novels, newspaper editorials, and historical documents. In a visually dominant culture, students need to learn visual discrimination with the same critical acumen they traditionally have approached literary works or other verbal documents. The analysis of the moving image, like the analysis of the written word, requires that we dissect the syntax of images (their narrative flow, their linear relations) and the semantics of images (their metaphorical associations, their referential beckoning to other realms of experience).

The fundamental problem is that the humanities and social sciences have not yet caught up with the actual practice of cultural reading in the late twentieth century. Text-bound disciplines feel uncomfortable with film and other visual media as primary source materials, when they are not actually opposed to their use. It is also obvious that philologically trained faculty lack a separate vocabulary and methodology to analyze visual texts that have become significant to the intellectual concerns of their disciplines.

The academy's current unease with film is a new wrinkle in the troubled history of the relation of word to image. Throughout the history of Western poetics, philosophers, writers and critics have recognized that linguistic and visual discourses are not mutually exclusive ways of representing the world and man's relationship to it. Still the line of demarcation between them has been complicated and frequently controversial. For example, classical treatises on rhetorical figures frequently referred to poetry as a kind of talking picture. In medieval scribal culture, many literary texts contained graphical illustrations as part of the manuscript; and in fine printed editions of the modern era, visual scenes serving as chapter heads or interludes between poems became almost a necessary condition of the book's definition.

In a converse sense, film criticism has had to rely heavily upon language, most particularly the interpretive tools of linguistic analysis. Christian Metz's seminal treatise on film is entitled *Language and Cinema* and his thesis about the conventions of film builds upon the theoretical paradigm of structural linguistics. And in actual cinematographic practice, the written script and the verbal soundtrack have proven to be as critical to successful films as the beautiful images captured by the motion picture camera. Perhaps it is worth remarking in this context that film first entered the academy in a major way through literature departments and through courses designed to compare cinematographic representations of literary masterworks to their original form of expression. The uneasy alliance between language and image was therefore reconfirmed.

Where the study of images has fallen very short of language study in college curricula is explicit training in the processes of visual communication. From the beginning of our educational experience, we are exposed to both reading and writing. It is assumed that the two dimensions of verbal proficiency go together, that each reinforces the other, and that mastery of both reading and writing sharpens critical awareness. In the curricular uses of film (except in film departments), the teaching of visual communication skills is almost non-existent. A central concern of our Luce Program is whether students and faculty can become truly literate in a visual sense without an understanding of and direct experience in the processes and techniques of visual representation.

Another curricular shortcoming is the uses to which films are put. Professors frequently approach film as unmediated content, as a kind of transparent window onto the intellectual preoccupations of history or anthropology or political science. This uncritical view of film substitutes the so-called ''documentary'' for reality (e.g., the historical event, the remote culture, or the social injustice) and assumes that the camera offers a transparent disclosure of the world instead of another layer of interpretation of events. The visual document, like the written text, is an uneasy mixture of fact and fiction and ideology, even in such experimental movements as the cinema verite of the 1960s.

Through the Luce Program in Cinema, Literacy and Culture, we believe that film can play a pedagogical role in the development of visual competency by drawing attention not only to what images have to say, but how they express that content. A sophisticated approach to visual media must get beyond the we-were-there attitude of historical documentaries and ethnographic films; it must confront the fact that films are reductive versions of raw footage, which itself came into being by the selective acts of the person behind the camera. This more technical and formal approach to visual literacy recognizes that film constructs meaning and offers a point of view. The special potency of films and other visual media is that they open our minds to new ways of seeing the world and that they impose upon us new perceptual experiences. Illusion is central to their power. Films may seek to capture reality as it is, but they also make familiar objects unfamiliar again (e.g., the effect of the zoom lens) by exposing their unnoticed aspects and renewing their significance.

Alfred Hitchcock's *The Birds* offers an interesting case study of film as illusion, a kind of visual parable about truth. Ostensibly, the film is a coming-to-terms with a mysterious and terrifying act of nature: huge flocks of birds descend upon a tranquil northern California coastal community and launch a campaign of terror by turning physically aggressive, destroying property, and actually killing people. At one level, the film is an ironic fable about the chaotic, unpredictable, and disruptive forces of nature, a moral tale of nature's unnaturalness.

At another level, *The Birds*, like Antonioni's *Blow-Up*, is one of the most overtly self-reflexive films about the nature of cinema and its power to effect a transforming vision. A central motif that recurs throughout the movie is the scene of a spectator before a window confronting an event that he or she cannot believe. In Hitchcock's thriller, the platitude that seeing is believing is turned upside down. In a pivotal scene of the movie, the cafe window in the village square becomes the frame for Melanie and Mitch's recounting of recent attacks by hostile birds. As members of the community express disbelief about these acts of violence and as the town's resident ornithologist offers scientific reassurances of normative avian behavior, the visual landscape outside begins to confirm Melanie and Mitch's tale. Birds amass; violent acts follow. When the the unbelievers finally turn toward the window, they witness events that their eyesight confirms but that their conceptual powers cannot comprehend. As the scene ends, the townsfolk are cowering in a corner opposite the window and, with appropriate symbolism, covering their eyes in terror.

In fact, the window or its substitute is the archetypal scene of violence throughout the movie. Image after image shows the birds flocking to a window and then aggressively crashing through this transparent and supposedly protective medium. There are the broken window panes of Mitch's house, the shattered glass telephone booth in the town square that momentarily imprisons Melanie, the trampled eyeglasses of the children running from the village school, and the shattered windshields of cars as townspeople try to flee inland. The suggestive power of these images is that the citizens' illusions have been shattered too. When Mitch's mother discovers the dead farmer, the physical evidence finally confirms, even surpasses, her worst imaginings : the shattered window pane on the bedroom floor and the pecked out eyes of the farmer (the ultimate violation of sight) point to the danger of the birds.

In the final scene of the movie, Melanie continues to flail her hands helplessly in front of her eyes even after she has been dragged from the bird-infested attic and the birds themselves no longer pose a physical threat to her safety. Melanie has succumbed to another order of vision, a paranoid fixation on imaginary birds. She refuses to accept the evidence of her own eyes or the verbal reassurances of the people around her that the birds have departed.

Melanie's experience has a parallel in our experience as spectators of the film. The film makes us re-evaluate whether the birds are real or imaginary. What exactly did we see? What can we really believe? From this vantage point, *The Birds* is not simply a movie about an inexplicable act of nature but a self-conscious exploration of the powers of illusion and a metaphor for cinema itself.

The purpose of this kind of reading is to suggest that the academy must also attempt to see film not simply as an exercise in content, but as a form of expression and as a self-reflexive act of communication. The Luce Program in Cinema, Literacy and Culture can function in a similar manner to achieve heightened awareness of visual communication and its consequences for literacy.

We propose through the Luce Program to explore visual media in three distinct areas of inquiry: film as theory, film as production, and film as document. To provide adequate coverage of these topics, we will bring in successive years three distinguished visiting scholars (Appendix A) to the Vassar campus to lead faculty seminars and to participate in new courses focussing on these aspects of film . In the first year, a scholar may concentrate on theoretical aspects of narrative film and the critical tools needed to analyze images and their effects. In the second year, we would seek an expert in production techniques who would direct campus discussion on the technical underpinnings of successful films. In the third year, a scholar bridging the concerns of theory and production would stimulate investigations of non-narrative films and their power to represent or misrepresent a world -- some aspect of reality as we know it.

All Luce Professors will share a common set of teaching and other scholarly responsibilities. Each will lead a faculty seminar on one of the three major thrusts of our program. Each will participate in the development and teaching of a film-based College Course. Each will offer an advanced film course related to his or her expertise. And each will develop a public program of films and lectures revolving around some aspect of the annual topic. Our budget request reflects these priorities (Appendix B). The final departmental affiliation of the Luce Professor will be determined by the scholar's field of expertise; one option may be a joint appointment in the Film Program (Appendix C) and the College Course Program (Appendix D).

In the faculty seminar program, the Luce Professor will serve as a catalyst for faculty development. While the theme may change yearly, the common agenda for the seminar series will be an opportunity for faculty to acquire the critical tools or technical knowledge needed for teaching film both as a central object of instruction (e. g., film as the primary text) and as an extension of other disciplinary work (e.g., film as social document). Each seminar will be composed of six or more instructors from different disciplines who may meet regularly during the academic year or organize an intensive summer workshop. Typical activities will include in-depth analyses of a few films, chosen to reflect the expertise of the visiting Luce Professor and the scholarly interests of the Vassar faculty in a genre, a period, or a production technique. Each Vassar participant will be responsible for bringing the methodological concerns of his or her discipline (historical, formal, philosophical, psychoanalytic, sociological, semiotic, ethnographic) to the study of particular films. Some theoretical readings are expected to parallel the detailed analysis of individual films. As a result of the seminar experience, Vassar faculty will be expected to incorporate the newly acquired cinematographic perspectives into their own courses and to be ambassadors to other colleagues.

At the end of the second year, one visiting Luce Professor would organize a special workshop that goes beyond the normal activities of the faculty seminar. This workshop would include hands-on experience with camera techniques, editing processes, sound mixing and other production processes. The premise underscoring this activity is not to develop faculty members as expert filmmakers but to enhance their understanding of the technical components of the process. As a natural outgrowth, the production of films and videos could begin to assume, as writing already does, an important place in the educational system as a recognized form of expression. The logical conduit for this special program would be the annual Powerhouse summer film workshop, which is under the direction of Vassar faculty and resident artists and which offers in-depth training in film to undergraduates under professional conditions.

As part of their curricular responsibilities, the Luce Professors will take an active role in the development of new film-related offerings in the College Course Program, whose purpose is to introduce students to interdisciplinary and integrative learning through analysis of significant cultural institutions from a variety of methodological and disciplinary perspectives. One proposed course would focus on ''The World of Images.'' Its central thrust is to introduce students to the reading of static and moving images and to offer a critical appraisal of their place and function in contemporary society. The first section of the course would study images from historical, philosophical and psychological perspectives. Topics may include the mental formation of images, the role of images in religion and ritual, and the relationship between visual icons and writing. The second part of the course would study sociological manifestations of visual communication today in advertising, film, television and other media. A second College Course would focus on ''Narrative Forms and the Media of Expression.'' Its central concern is comparative analysis of the function and form of narrative. Structurally, the course could be organized around the ''epic'' accounts of a people's or a nation's identity in various cultures at different periods of history. Primary materials might include written epics, such as the *Iliad* and the *Aeneid* in the classical period of western civilization; recorded oral stories, such as the mythological tales of North and South American native peoples; musical opera in modern Italian and German civilization; western films in recent American society; and soap operas and serial films in the developing nations of India and Egypt.

As part of their public outreach, the Luce Professors will be asked to organize an annual film and lecture series around a major theme of their year-long program. This series of film screenings would dovetail with a parallel set of public lectures that would address theoretical concerns or technical aspects of the selected films. For example, in the third year, the Luce Professor may organize a program of war movies, war documentaries, and news broadcasts as a point of departure for comparing the techniques of various visual media and their differing representations of fact and fiction. The series might also explore the role of ideology -- for example, the depiction of heroism -- in the selection and arrangement of war images. As another example, a film series might trace the evolution of cinematographic representations of women in American culture. A parallel lecture series could then analyze the celluloid depiction and compare the fictional prototypes of heroine, mother, daughter, wife, and career woman to the sociological reality of women's place in the world at that time.

Through the faculty seminars, the production workshop, the curricular initiatives, and the public film series, Vassar proposes with the assistance of visiting Luce Professors to explore the medium of film as an opening onto larger issues of communication and literacy. It is not our intention to give the Luce Program departmental autonomy and thus isolate its intellectual concerns from the broader issues of the liberal arts, nor is it our wish to circumscribe the medium's social impact by limiting discussion to the synergistic powers of the creative arts. We view the conjunction of cinema, literacy and culture as a deliberate attempt to recognize visual technology as a powerful means of expression for transmitting all kinds of knowledge and depicting many forms of reality. In the late twentieth century, film and its allied visual media are becoming what the book and the newspaper have been for several centuries of print culture. We must accept and understand this revolution and its consequences. It is in this sense that film bears enormous consequences, at once threatening and promising, for the future of literacy and culture. We believe the Luce Program can contribute significantly to this debate within the academy.

BUDGET REQUEST
LUCE PROGRAM IN CINEMA, LITERACY AND CULTURE

Visiting Professor

$75,000 X 3 years $225,000

    salary
    fringe benefits
    relocation allowance

Faculty Seminar

$6,500 X 3 years $19,500

    faculty honoraria
    program expenses for films, books,
    photocopying, and hospitality

Summer Production Workshop

$45,000 X 1 summer $45,000

    faculty honoraria
    technical consultants
    equipment purchase /rental
    materials and supplies

Public Film / Lecture Series

$3,500 X 3 years $10,500

    film rentals
    visiting lecturers
    programs expenses
        hospitality
        publicity
        audio/visual charges

TOTAL BUDGET $300,000

Success with a Corporation I:
Gallaudet Makes a Case for a Special Constituency

The Institution: Gallaudet University is the world's only accredited four-year liberal arts university where programs and services are geared specifically for deaf and hard of hearing students. All pre-college and undergraduate students are deaf or hard of hearing students. Gallaudet also offers graduate programs for both deaf and hearing students in professions serving deaf and hard of hearing individuals. Founded in 1864, Gallaudet is a diagnostic center, a preschool, an elementary school, a high school, a research institution, a national treasure house of information on deafness, an international training center, and an undergraduate and graduate degree-granting university. Tens of thousands of individuals, including deaf adults, their families and co-workers, and professionals in deafness-related fields, are served worldwide each year through a variety of University outreach programs.

The Author: Ms. Catherine Dehoney, Director of Corporate and Foundation Relations at Gallaudet, wrote this proposal in collaboration with Dr. James R. Speegle, Dean of the School of Management at Gallaudet University.

Ms. Dehoney joined the staff of Gallaudet in 1991. In writing the GE proposal, she worked closely with Dr. Speegle. Prior to her current position, she was Director of Annual Giving at the American Symphony Orchestra League in Washington, D.C. During her tenure at the League she also served as Interim Director of Development, Associate Director of Corporate Giving, and Development Writer. She received her B.A. from the College of William and Mary in 1983.

Background: The GE Foundation had made one prior grant to Gallaudet University before its gift in 1992 under the GE Faculty For the Future Program. In 1988, the University received a gift of $25,000 to support entrepreneurial studies programs in Gallaudet's newly established School of Management.

EXECUTIVE SUMMARY

Gallaudet University, the world's only four-year liberal arts university for deaf and hard of hearing students, is honored to be invited to apply for a grant under the General Electric Foundation's Faculty for the Future program. Gallaudet requests a grant of $100,000 over three years to be used to encourage current business faculty and teaching assistants to complete advanced degrees through a combined release time/forgivable loan program.

Until recently, deaf people have had difficulty obtaining managerial positions in the private or public sector. With the implementation of the Americans with Disabilities Act (ADA), new career and social opportunities are opening for deaf and hard of hearing people. As the leading institution of higher learning for deaf people and as a focal point of deaf culture, Gallaudet University must provide its students with the highest quality education possible so that they can compete and succeed in whatever fields they choose.

Gallaudet's School of Management plays an important role in preparing deaf people to participate fully in the business world. Our students look to their instructors/professors to serve as mentors and to set examples for their professional lives. Given the close-knit nature of the deaf community, deaf role models, particularly women and minority individuals, are of critical importance in any effort to encourage deaf people's full participation in American business. The GE Faculty for the Future grant would enable Gallaudet to help develop its faculty by encouraging their attainment of graduate and doctoral degrees.

Because the University's primary focus is on teaching and professional development, Ph.D. attainment is not necessarily a requirement for new professors. Gallaudet plans to establish a release time/forgivable loan program: Faculty who have not yet obtained doctoral degrees and teaching assistants who are pursuing graduate degrees will be given either release time of one-fourth to one-half of their teaching obligations or direct financial loans to assist in completing their dissertations or graduate studies. Once they have obtained their degree, they would be expected to continue working in a teaching position at a college or university business school. For each year they are employed in this way, the value of their release time or direct loan will be forgiven at a rate of 25 percent.

The University has identified several candidates who would meet the criteria for the program, including several women and minority graduate students. By helping our faculty and graduate students obtain their advanced degrees, Gallaudet will be developing highly qualified deaf faculty members whose skills can be put to immediate good use for our undergraduate students. We believe that this program will provide strong role models and mentors for future deaf business professionals.

45

New Expectations: Preparing Deaf and Hard of Hearing Students for Increased Professional Opportunities

For more than 125 years, Gallaudet University has been the premier institution of higher learning serving deaf and hard of hearing people through education, research, and public service. Now, extraordinary changes are taking place at Gallaudet and throughout the deaf community. Recent events, including the appointment of Gallaudet's first deaf president and the implementation of the Americans with Disabilities Act (ADA), have irreversibly changed the University and the American workplace. The expectations of our students have been raised to new heights. The majority of earlier alumni prepared themselves to work in a few professions such as teaching and printing. Today, when asked what they want to do when they graduate, students tell us they want to be doctors, lawyers, computer programmers, journalists, or corporate executives.

Gallaudet is working to strengthen its programs to help prepare deaf students for the opportunities opening to them. Having excelled for over a century at educating deaf students, most of whom used their skills and talents within the deaf community, Gallaudet now must use its expertise to educate more deaf people who will take their places as leaders and participants in the broad spectrum of American life.

The School of Management: Educating Deaf Students for Successful Careers in Business

The School of Management was established in 1987 to meet high student interest and strong demand in the public and private sectors of the business community. In the four years since the School was founded, the number of students enrolling in business courses has increased by 30 percent. This year, 30 percent of graduating seniors have declared majors in the School of Management. The undergraduate programs of the School of Management are designed to prepare students for direct entry into careers in business, or government, or for graduate study in business, economics, law, public administration, and similar fields. Students may elect the following majors:

> Accounting
> Business Administration (with concentrations in
>   Management or Entrepreneurial Studies)
> Computer Information Systems
> Economics

In addition to their college courses, most of our students take advantage of work/study programs. These internships provide valuable, hands-on training, which give our students the edge they need to compete for jobs in various industries.

The School of Management has also developed programs that reach out to the business community to promote career advancement, leadership, and entrepreneurship by deaf and hard of hearing people. These programs are a part of the Management Institute.

The Essential Role of Faculty in Encouraging the Development of Deaf Business Professionals

While Gallaudet does at this time offer advanced degrees in business, it is the academic and cultural hub of the deaf community. Often called the ''Harvard'' of deaf education and the ''mecca'' for deaf people, Gallaudet offers deaf students a barrier-free environment, where communication is clear and comfortable. If deaf people in greater numbers are going to become leaders in American society, it is Gallaudet that will provide them with the highest quality education and support in their professional lives. Thus, Gallaudet's School of Management has a unique opportunity to encourage deaf people's participation in both academia and in private enterprise.

As professional opportunities increasingly become open to deaf people, the School of Management faculty will play an even more important role in the preparation of deaf students and the advancement of our graduates. Until recently, there have not been many deaf professionals in management or pursuing entrepreneurial endeavors. Our students look to their instructors to serve as mentors and to set examples for their professional lives. Given the close-knit nature of the deaf community, deaf role models, particularly women and minority individuals, are of critical importance in any effort to encourage deaf people's full participation in American business.

As in our society at large, deaf women and minority individuals face even more challenges in reaching their professional goals. The nationwide effort to increase the number of minority and women professors on the business faculty is made even more complex at Gallaudet by the additional dimension of deafness. Currently, the School of Management faculty is 63 percent deaf, 25 percent women, and 25 percent African-American, Asian, and Hispanic. There are 16 full-time faculty and 6-8 part-time faculty and teaching assistants. The School of Management has established Affirmative Action goals for increasing women and minority faculty members to the level of 40 percent and 33 percent respectively. As it works to reach these goals, the School of Management is fortunate to have a strong group of students. Of the 200+ students who have declared majors within the School of Management, all are deaf or hard of hearing. Approximately 44 percent are women and 13 percent are minority individuals.

˙ Proposal: A Program to
Develop Highly Qualified, Diverse Business Faculty

One of the University's highest priorities in promoting excellence throughout its curricula is faculty development programs. Because of the relatively limited role deaf people have played in the business world, the University is particularly interested in helping to prepare highly qualified business professors and role models for its students by encouraging the attainment of advanced degrees. Gallaudet is primarily a teaching university, although state-of-the-art research is conducted in areas related to deafness and deaf education. As in other schools at the University, the School of Management focuses on teaching and professional preparation rather than research. Therefore, Ph.D. attainment in the past has not necessarily been a prerequisite for new faculty in business.

Gallaudet University requests a grant of $100,000 over three years from the GE Foundation's Faculty for the Future Program to establish a forgivable loan program. This program will help to prepare and encourage talented deaf faculty and associate teachers, particularly women and minority individuals, to complete their doctoral studies or other graduate degrees.

The dean of the School of Management will identify individuals who are currently serving as full-time and part-time faculty or teaching assistants and who have demonstrated a strong interest in pursuing a career in academia. The appropriate candidates will be deaf and have either started graduate degree programs or have shown strong interest in pursuing such study. Preference will be given to women and culturally diverse candidates.

Depending on their teaching and faculty responsibilities, these individuals will be offered one-fourth to one-half release time from their teaching obligations for one year to provide additional time to pursue graduate study or to complete dissertations. The program will be similar to the model used by many universities in their sabbatical agreements, in which the faculty member must agree to continue working at the university for a specific period of time or pay back the salary paid during the sabbatical leave. Under Gallaudet's program, the release time will become a forgivable loan, equivalent to the percentage of the faculty member's salary represented by the release time (i.e. 25 percent, 33 percent). We expect to offer up to five forgivable loans each year, consideration of release time, direct loans, or a combination of the two. The GE Foundation grant will enable Gallaudet to hire appropriate teaching support to cover those classes affected under the release time program.

In requiring such ''work-study'', Gallaudet will be helping to provide the faculty-students with a supportive environment among deaf and hearing colleagues. For less-experienced teachers working as part-time faculty or assistants, the program will give them the opportunity to earn their advanced degrees while working in their chosen field under the tutelage of experienced mentors. Gallaudet gains role models for its undergraduate students as well as better-prepared teaching/research assistants and additional faculty members with competitive credentials competitive with their colleagues at other university programs.

The candidate will be expected to complete all requirements for their degree within a specified time frame. For a master's degree this will be four years, and for a doctoral degree, the maximum time frame would be six years. After the individual has received a graduate degree, the loan would be forgiven at a rate of 25 percent for each year of full-time service as a member of a college or university faculty-- Gallaudet or another institution of higher learning. The program will be administered by the Dean of the School of Management in conjunction with the Provost. Ideally, the program will begin in the fall semester of 1992.

To determine the effectiveness of this program, the University will use its established evaluation process for faculty members. It is expected that these teachers acquiring advanced study will demonstrate more skill and creativity in their instructional methods and curriculum development. There is no dearth of potential candidates for the fellowship program. Gallaudet has identified three potential candidates among its business faculty members. Each of these has begun a graduate program applicable to business education. We are also aware of three promising African-American graduate students and one senior female undergraduate who have the desire and interest to be successful in this program. Two of the graduate students are at the University of Maryland: one, a woman, is in her first year of an M.B.A. program, and the other, a man, is working on his doctorate in Management Information Systems. The third is a man, pursuing a master's degree in Instructional Technology at Gallaudet. All have expressed interest in staying at Gallaudet and working with the deaf community.

Not only will this gift serve as significant encouragement to talented deaf faculty and graduate students in business, it will also have a multiplier effect as these individuals succeed and go out into the larger community. As role models and qualified teachers in higher education, these business experts will encourage countless other deaf women and minority individuals to pursue their professional goals and go on to make valuable contributions to American society.

Publicity

Should the GE Foundation choose to fund Gallaudet's forgivable loan program, the University will be pleased to name the program the General Electric Forgivable Loan program. We would publicize the awarding of the grant in the Chronicle of

Higher Education and journals related to philanthropy including the Chronicle of Philanthropy and the Nonprofit Times. In addition, we would announce the establishment of this program in various newspapers that are circulated to the deaf community nationwide and in educational journals related to deafness.

Gallaudet Background

Chartered by Abraham Lincoln in 1864, Gallaudet University is a multipurpose educational institution and resource center that serves deaf and hard of hearing people around the world through a full range of academic, research, and public service programs. Each year, more than 2,200 students from all 50 states, the District of Columbia, and 59 foreign countries come to matriculate at Gallaudet. The University offers more than 40 undergraduate and graduate programs leading to A.A., A.A.S., B.A., B.S., M.A., M.S., ED.S, and Ph.D. degrees through five schools: Arts and Sciences; Education and Human Services--currently celebrating its centennial; Preparatory Studies; Communication; and the newest, the School of Management. Additionally, innovative precollege programs at the Kendall Demonstration Elementary School and the Model Secondary School for the Deaf serve over 600 students.

Although deaf and hard of hearing students are welcome at many other colleges and universities across the nation, Gallaudet is the only university in the world where they have full access, where communication is not a barrier in the classroom or in their social or pre-professional life. Deaf students can participate directly and take advantage of communication that is clear and comfortable. At Gallaudet, the playing field is level; deafness is the norm.

Gallaudet's influence extends far beyond its two campuses in Washington, D.C. Tens of thousands of individuals nationwide and internationally are served through a variety of University outreach programs and services including six regional extension centers, the National Information Center on Deafness, the Gallaudet Research Institute, and the International Center on Deafness. The following statistics demonstrate the scope of Gallaudet's service and educational accomplishments.

A.   More than 70 percent of all profoundly deaf people with a college degree are Gallaudet graduates.

B.   85 percent of Gallaudet graduates are employed in professional, technical, and managerial occupations.

C.   More than 63 percent of Gallaudet University graduates pursue advanced degrees.

GENERAL ELECTRIC/GALLAUDET UNIVERSITY
FORGIVABLE LOAN PROGRAM

SUGGESTED GUIDELINES FOR LOAN AGREEMENT

The recipient agrees to repay 1) an amount equal to the percentage of salary represented by the release time agreement AND/OR 2) an amount directly financed by the University upon any of the following events:

The recipient ceases to be an employee at any time within one year following the date of the loan disbursement or release-time period.

The recipient does not satisfactorily complete the graduate degree for which educational assistance was given. It is expected that master's degrees will be completed within four years and doctoral degrees completed within six years.

The recipient ceases to be enrolled as a graduate student at a four-year accredited American college or university.

Cancellation Policy for Teaching:

If the recipient has received a graduate degree and is employed in a teaching position or related position with a business school at a four-year accredited American college or university, the loan or release-time equivalent will be forgiven at a rate of 25% of the total amount borrowed for each year the recipient teaches on a full-time basis.

It is expected that the recipient will make a good faith effort to obtain employment in such a teaching position. The University will grant a grace period for the loan repayment of up to two years while the recipient seeks an appropriate teaching position.

GENERAL ELECTRIC/GALLAUDET UNIVERSITY
FORGIVABLE LOAN PROGRAM
BUDGET

YEAR	RECIPIENTS	AMT/RECIPIENT	TOTAL
1	1-3 Tenure Track Faculty 1-3 Part-Time Faculty	$7-10,000	$34,000
2	1-3 Tenure Track Faculty 1-3 Part-Time Faculty	$7-10,000	$33,000
3	1-3 Tenure Track Faculty 1-3 Part-Time Faculty	$7-10,000	$33,000

STRATEGY

The GE/Gallaudet Program would provide forgivable loans for two types of candidates. Up to three deaf, tenure-track faculty members would each be given a loan of $7,000-$10,000 per year for each of three years.

The loan could be accepted in addition to on-going compensation for teaching responsibilities. Candidates who accepted the loan in addition to salary would be those whose need was primarily for financial assistance to help with tuition, fees, and expenses.

Alternatively, the loan could be used to provide partial release from teaching responsibilities. Candidates who chose this option would be those who wanted to increase the time available to them for taking classes, doing research, and writing. Candidates could combine these two options.

Similar loans of $7-10,000 would be available for up to three deaf, part-time faculty. These individuals would be selected for their outstanding ability and for their demonstrated interest in preparing for academic careers in business. Gallaudet would provide the candidates with part-time teaching assignments in order to assure the availability of an intellectually rich peer professional support group.

These part-time faculty would also have the option of accepting the forgivable loan as an addition to teaching compensation or combining the two options.

Goal: **To increase the number of qualified, business professors, particularly women and minorities, by encouraging current tenure-track and part-time faculty to complete advanced degrees.**

Objective I: To Provide Peer Professional Support

The GE/Gallaudet Program would enable the aspiring degree recipient to continue teaching at Gallaudet at least part-time. Thus, the program would assure a collegial group of fellow professors and advanced students who are fluent in American Sign Language and have common professional and academic interests.

In any advanced graduate program, peer support is an essential ingredient for success. An aspiring degree recipient needs challenging colleagues with whom to discuss thesis and dissertation ideas. Later this peer support group will discuss theories, problems, analytical issues, writing blocks, literature surveys, and the like. Although hearing graduate students have multiple opportunities to participate in formal and informal discussions with professors and fellow students, deaf graduate students in other colleges are often encumbered by the need to work through an interpreter. This requires that discussions be scheduled and that discussion group members be sensitive to the added protocols of working with an interpreter.

Objective II: To Provide Financial Support

The GE/Gallaudet Program would provide support for tuition, books, fees, and living expenses, including transportation and child care needs.

Success with a Corporation II:
Interlochen Offers A New View of the Bottom Line

The Institution: Interlochen Center for the Arts includes the Interlochen Arts Camp, the Interlochen Arts Academy and Interlochen Public Radio. The Center is located on a 1,200 acre campus in the northwest section of Michigan's lower peninsula.

Interlochen Arts Camp, chartered in 1927, is the oldest and most successful summer arts program for artists ages 8 to 18. Accelerated instruction in music, theater, dance and visual arts attracts students from every state and more than 30 countries.

Founded in 1962, the Interlochen Arts Academy is the premier fine arts boarding high school. Music, theater, dance, visual arts, creative writing and college preparatory academics are offered to students in grades 9 through 12.

A charter member of National Public Radio, Interlochen Public Radio is owned and operated by Interlochen Center for the Arts.

The Author: Marsha Smith is currently the Director of the Annual Fund at Interlochen Center for the Arts. She and a staff of two others are responsible for raising over $3 million each year. Corporate and Foundation contributions make up over 35% of the total dollars raised annually. When this proposal was submitted in 1991, Ms. Smith was the Associate Director of Corporate and Foundation Relations. She has been in the field of development for 12 years, 5 of these at Interlochen.

Background: Interlochen corporate staff began cultivating the Monsanto Corporation in 1990. The relationship began with a personal call to the Community Relations Coordinator at corporate headquarters in St. Louis. This meeting resulted in a proposal being submitted for minority student scholarships, which was subsequently funded. During the summer of 1990 the Monsanto representative visited Interlochen's campus and met with scholarship recipients. This 1991 proposal is a request for renewal of the minority student grant. It was funded Support for the program continues.

March 20, 1991

Dr. John Mason
President
The Monsanto Fund
800 North Landers Blvd.
St. Louis, MO 63167

Dear Dr. Mason:

Interlochen Center for the Arts has appreciated previous support from the Monsanto Fund. It is now my honor to submit the enclosed proposal requesting continuing consideration of the minority scholarship program with a grant in the range of $5,000. The Monsanto Fund gift will be used to provide at least two scholarships for minority students from Monsanto operating locations to attend Interlochen Arts Camp 1991.

A summer at Interlochen Arts Camp (formerly National Music Camp) can be a life changing experience for a young person. In this unique international atmosphere students from all cultures, economic backgrounds, races and religions come together and learn many important life lessons. One of the most important and perhaps most difficult may be learning to combine competition and cooperation to achieve personal objectives and group goals. This is a lesson learned every day in orchestra, band, dance ensembles and theatre productions.

The enclosed proposal outlines our program in more detail. We hope that the Monsanto Corporation will join with other national corporations underwriting the minority scholarship program at Interlochen including the Kellogg Company, the Dayton Hudson Foundation, the Chrysler Fund and Pacific Telesis Foundation. If you should have any questions about the enclosed proposal, please do not hesitate to contact me.

Thank you for your continuing consideration.

Sincerely,

Marsha Smith
Associate Director of Development
for Corporate Relations

WINNING GRANT PROPOSALS

PROPOSAL TO MONSANTO CORPORATION

In a time when corporations are responding to national problems such as the crisis in public education, an increasing population of hungry and homeless, and a national drug epidemic, why should they support the arts? Because the arts help individuals and groups transcend their desperation, think creatively about solutions, and communicate feelings, emotions, and fears in a variety of ways. Without the arts all of our lives would be diminished and without corporate support of the arts the quality of our communities would be lessened.

Many corporations, like Monsanto, recognize this and support orchestras, operas, dance troupes, museums and galleries in their hometowns. So why should they consider funding an arts education institution in northern Michigan? Aside from the fact that without Interlochen there might be empty chairs in orchestras, missed arias, vacant stages, and bare gallery walls nationwide, the importance of Interlochen lies in the specialized training, a training that cannot be replicated in individual communities.

At Interlochen young people from around the globe gather to share their love of the arts and develop their skills. In this accelerated international atmosphere students gain self-assurance and learn problem solving skills. In a very practical way they learn the fine art of balancing competition and cooperation, an important lesson in the band and the board room.

For years Interlochen Center for the Arts has served as our nation's premier pre-professional arts institution. Students from ages 8 - 22 from each of the states and around the world have studied, developed, and grown during the summers at Interlochen Arts Camp (formerly National Music Camp) and throughout the school year at Interlochen Arts Academy. All of the major symphony orchestras nationwide contain at least 10% Interlochen alumni. The St. Louis Symphony orchestra has over 7 members who have attended Interlochen. A list is attached.

Yet most of our 41,000 alumni are now involved in disciplines other than the arts. The lessons they learn amongst the music and trees of the north woods are important life lessons that help them become well-rounded individuals and often leaders in their own communities. Innovative balanced leadership for communities through the world is another real benefit of Interlochen and a "pay off" for corporations who invest their dollars in talented young people.

OUR REQUEST

Interlochen Center for the Arts requests renewed support from the Monsanto Corporation with a grant in the range of $5,000. This gift will be used to provide scholarship assistance to low income minority children from Monsanto operating locations, enabling them to attend Interlochen Arts Camp 1991.

COMMITMENT TO ACCESS AND OPPORTUNITY

Interlochen has long been dedicated to providing opportunities to excel in the arts for children of all races, colors, and creeds. Interlochen's founder, Joseph E. Maddy, believed that music and the arts were a "universal language" that dissolved social, economic, and geographic barriers.

This initial dedication to world friendship and equality is currently being expanded and strengthened. In order to continue significantly increasing minority enrollments, Interlochen must become even more effective in searching our talented students and securing additional dollars for financial aid.

We can only do this with the help and support of corporations like Monsanto Corporation and others who continue to fund minority student scholarships. Other donors include: The Skillman Foundation; Kellogg Company; Dayton Hudson Foundation; Montgomery Ward and Company, Inc.; The Botwinick-Wolfensohn Foundation; The Xerox Foundation; Chrysler Fund; and The Pacific Telesis Foundation.

Many of the minority students who have attended the Interlochen Arts Camp and the Interlochen Arts Academy have gone on to assume leadership roles in the arts. A few examples are: Jessye Norman, star of the Metropolitan Opera; Wendell Harris, Jr., film maker and video producer; Darwyn Apple, member of St. Louis Symphony and featured soloist; Richard Robinson, newest member of the Detroit Symphony Orchestra and Damon Evans of the Metropolitan Opera and television show "The Jeffersons."

SCHOLARSHIP SUPPORT

Nearly 22% of all the students at the Interlochen Arts Camp and 67% of all students enrolled at the Interlochen Arts Academy receive scholarship support. The percentage of minority students receiving financial aid is higher, with 42% of the minority campers receiving aid and 68% of the minority students at the Academy on scholarship assistance. Overall, $2,025,000 in financial assistance was awarded in Fiscal Year 1990, 25% of this went to minority students.

Only 40% of this total financial aid budget is funded by the endowment. The balance must be raised through annual contributions. The majority of funds provided for low income students comes from corporations and foundations, like Monsanto.

The Monsanto Fund scholarship fund will be allocated to artistically qualified minority students from your operating locations. Scholarship allocation will be based upon each individual child's family situation. Monsanto funds may be used

WINNING GRANT PROPOSALS

to help provide the cost of transportation and other Camp related expenses in cases where the family is without any personal financial resources. Determination of allocations will be made by the Admissions Department of Interlochen Arts Camp.

CORPORATE SUPPORT

Corporate support for Interlochen Center for the Arts has been growing dramatically over the past few years. In part, this derives from a growing appreciation by corporate executives for the arts and for the contributions the arts make to communities in which businesses function. Additionally, it has been nourished by the group of executives on the Interlochen Center for the Arts National Corporate Council.

The National Corporate Council was begun in 1985 to:

- Increase the corporate community's knowledge of Interlochen
- Increase corporate financial support for Interlochen
- Enhance Interlochen's national and international reputation

Today there are 31 members representing major corporations across the United States. Corporate giving totaled over $784,000 is Fiscal Year 1989-1990.

CORPORATE SCHOLARSHIP RECOGNITION

Media Recognition

1. Press release to print media in key locations announcing establishment of the scholarship and providing details on how to apply

2. Announcement of scholarship recipient to same print media

3. Release on recipient's honors or awards achieved

4. Public service announcements to radio and TV stations as appropriate, announcing scholarship availability, etc.

Interlochen recognition

1. Listing in Interlochen Arts Academy admission packet of scholarship opportunities

2. Listing in Interlochen Crescendo donor list

3. Listing in Interlochen's corporate brochure

4. Listing in Interlochen's annual report

Contact with student recipient

1. Notice of student recipient's name, address, age, and major emphasis of study

2. Letter from student recipient

3. Notice of student progress report

4. Meeting with student at the work place or on Interlochen's campus

5. Possible performance of student at corporate headquarters or designated work place

CONCLUSION

To achieve our goals we are requesting a grant in the range of $5,000 from the Monsanto Fund. Your gift will be used to provide at least 2 scholarships for designated minority students to attend Interlochen Arts Camp 1991.

We are convinced that minority scholarship assistance not only will benefit the students and Interlochen, but will also have a widespread long-term effect on the quality of life of our entire nation.

I will be pleased to provide additional information or answer any questions you may have about Interlochen.

_____   _____
Date   Dean Boal, President

Success with the Individual:
Lake Forest College Waits for the Right Time with Alumni

The Institution: Lake Forest College is a coeducational, undergraduate liberal arts institution founded in 1857 and located in suburban Lake Forest, Illinois, 28 miles north of Chicago. A member of the Associated Colleges of the Midwest, Lake Forest College boasts a highly qualified faculty and a 12:1 student-faculty ratio. Forty-five states and 23 foreign countries are represented in the College's student body of approximately 1,000. In 1987, Lake Forest College became the first small, liberal arts college in more than 20 years to be granted chapter status in Sigma Xi, the scientific honorary society. Lake Forest College also holds one of only nine Illinois chapters of Phi Beta Kappa.

The Author: Ann Shillinglaw is Director of Foundation and Corporate Relations at Lake Forest College. She is a 1981 graduate of Lake Forest College, and earned a Master's Degree in English Literature in 1983 from Syracuse University.

Background: The alumnus was identified as a major donor prospect. Until this point, he had given to the annual fund, but not for capital purposes. He was visited by the President of the College and, later, the Director of Development, who made a major gift solicitation. This proposal immediately followed that request.

A Proposal to Scott Fossel '75
to Endow a Student Leadership Fund
at Lake Forest College

As a small, high-quality liberal arts college, Lake Forest College is uniquely able to offer to the members of its diverse student body many opportunities to take on leadership roles. At Lake Forest College, these opportunities exist in close ratio to the number of students. Because the experience of leadership shapes character in a lasting way, the challenges and victories a student leader experiences make him or her a stronger member of society. Student leadership opportunities are an important part of student life at Lake Forest College, a critical addition to educational and athletic programs. As a committed Lake Forest College alumnus who served as student government president, you well understand the need for leadership opportunities and training for today's students. Lake Forest College respectfully requests that you make a gift of $100,000 to endow and name a Student Leadership Fund at Lake Forest College.

Student Leadership at Lake Forest College

The endowed fund, named as you wish, would support activities on campus which provide and promote leadership opportunities for students. At present, these activities include student government, the Red and Black student organization, the Senior 25, and the Freshman Leadership Series; and though other organizations will supplant some of these as time passes, there will always be opportunities at Lake Forest College for students to learn to lead.

Through these opportunities, Lake Forest College students, perhaps for the first time in their lives, perhaps drawing on secondary school experience, take in hand the challenges of leading others and bearing the responsibility for their own decisions which affect others. Student leaders learn to work together, regardless of race, background, or academic interest, for their common goals. With a full-time student population of 1049, of which all but 134 live on campus, Lake Forest College finds that its student leaders interact closely with the entire student body. The interaction between faculty and students and students with each other made possible by the College's size and emphasis on residential life produces student leaders who have learned to mediate, solve community problems, and juggle the demands of academic life with social and volunteer life.

While all extracurricular activity allows participants to savor the fruits of leadership, there are at present four organizations especially designed to heighten students' recognition that they themselves may lead. Those organizations are described below:

Student Government at Lake Forest College

The Lake Forest College student government has several functions. It administers the student activities annual budget of $135,000 to all student organizations on campus. In the process of allocating and supervising student funds, gathered through an annual student fee, student government leaders wrestle with the responsibility of prioritizing, equitably disbursing the monies, and assuring that they are wisely spent.

Student government also serves as the forum for student communication to administration and faculty on campus issues. At weekly student government meetings, students speak out on all issues that face them on the Lake Forest College campus, from curricular decisions to national student concerns.

In addition to keeping its doors open to all students, student government offers a unique position to its leaders. The president and vice president of the student government serve as members of the Lake Forest College Board of Trustees, participating in discussions and deciding issues critical to the life of the College alongside business and community leaders.

The Red and Black

While student government offers opportunities to lead to all students, the Red and Black organization gives academic leaders recognition and a sense of community by providing them with campus housing where they can live as a unit and run academically oriented programs in their residence hall. This organization, which also includes nonresident academic achievers, gives academic leaders a visible position on campus.

This year, 60 students applied to become Red and Black members, and 28 were chosen. Members of Red and Black must have a 3.0 grade point average and promote cultural and intellectual activities within the context of an academic support community. This organization sponsors faculty forums, trips to Chicago area events of an academic and cultural nature, and weekly lectures open to all students. Members of the group serve as role models of academic achievement and community for the campus.

The Senior 25

In addition to student government and the Red and Black, Lake Forest College students may be selected to the Senior 25 in recognition of their academic achievement, leadership qualities and their efforts in working positively in the

College community as exemplary role models. This year, 70 students were nominated for 25 positions. Being named one of the Senior 25 can have great impact on a student's life while he or she is a member of a small college community, and instill in that student a sense of leadership that will carry on into the larger world outside of campus.

The Freshman Leadership Series at Lake Forest College

In the fall of 1989, the College's Dean of Students office began offering leadership training to freshman students. Twenty-five freshmen participated in a series of five workshops run by staff and upperclassmen for discussion of leadership opportunities at the College and what it means to be a leader. Student government officers and trustees of Lake Forest College also participated. The Freshman Leadership Series teaches these beginning college students leadership skills and shows them they have the power to change things and to communicate effectively. All freshmen may study leaders in history, politics, psychology, sociology, and economics classrooms; the leadership training series prepares them to take on leadership responsibilities within the Lake Forest College community.

An Endowed Student Leadership Fund

An endowed fund for Student Leadership at Lake Forest College would assist the College in funding leadership activities on campus. Such an endowment would pay the expenses of Student Government, providing lasting support for student governance. An endowment of $100,000 would also make it possible to offset costs incurred by the Dean of Students' office in nominating and electing Senior 25 members. In addition, this endowment could be used to promote leadership on campus by offering stipends to special speakers at Red and Black Lectures and fund educational trips into the city of Chicago.

An endowment for student leadership could also enable leadership training sessions to include an off-campus retreat in which students from all four classes on campus could participate to create a better sense of community among the various campus organizations. Moreover, an endowment for student leadership will ensure the continuation of such leadership opportunities on the campus of Lake Forest College for future generations of students.

The Request

Lake Forest College seeks to educate its students not only in the liberal arts but in life experience. The College is proud to offer to its students the challenges of selfgovernment and the recognition of leadership through the Red and Black and

Senior 25. We respectfully offer you the opportunity to endow and name a fund for student leadership at Lake Forest College with a gift of $100,000. This student leadership fund may be named as you wish.

Leadership experience at the college level enables students to evolve into strong leaders later in life in their careers and communities. It would be particularly fitting that this fund for student leadership at Lake Forest College be endowed and perhaps named by an alumnus who himself experienced the challenges and rewards of student leadership while a student at Lake Forest College and who understands the impact of leadership opportunities on the lives of young people.

Success with the National Endowment for the Arts: Making the Application Work for the Dunham Centers

The Institution: The Katherine Dunham Centers were founded by Ms. Dunham in 1970 as the Dunham Fund for Research and Development of Cultural Ats. The organization promotes arts based communication for people of diverse cultures through a multi-arts training program.

The Author: Margaret Elliott is an award winning poet and essayist with over fifteen years of business writing experience. She began her career in nonprofit management and development at The Saint Louis Art Museum in 1986, after earning her M.B. A. from Washington University in St. Louis. In her seven years as a fund-raising professional, her proposals to government agencies, corporations and foundations have earned nearly $3 million for nonprofit clients. Ms. Elliott specializes in fund development for small to mid-size arts organizations. She also serves a wide variety of clients through NonProfit Network, a professional consulting partnership she co-founded in 1992 and assists commercial clients through her firm The Word Doctor, a professional writing service.

Background: This proposal was submitted to the Expansion Arts Program of the NEA by the Katherine Dunham Centers for Arts and Humanities in 1991 resulting in a grant of $40,000. Ms. Elliott offers the following general advice to grantwriters working on similar federal government proposals: ''1) Get to know you program specialist. The NEA and many other Federal agencies are staffed with friendly, accessible experts for each grant category. They can help you decide whether your program is eligible for funds, and guide you through the application process. If your proposal fails, they can tell you why so you can succeed next time, and, 2) Write your proposal from a client's perspective. The best programs serve people. Be specific about what needs you are meeting for your audience, who your clients are, and how many of them you reach.'' Ms. Elliott cites several people as being central to the success of this appeal, including ''Jeannelle Stovall, who contributed substantially to getting these ideas on paper and Katherine Dunham, who still inspires some of my best work.'' She also recognizes Dr. Cynthia Hardy for providing her with the opportunity to prepare this proposal for the Dunham Centers. She also identifies A.B. Spellman, Yvonne Rory and Patrice Powell, staff of the Expansion Arts Program. ''Finally,'' she writes, ''I would like to acknowledge the vision of former NEA chair Frank Hodsoll, whose enthusiasm for the Dunham Centers played a large role in their survival and present success.''

October 9, 1991

Ms. Patrice Powell
Program Specialist, Expansion Arts
National Endowment for the Arts
Nancy Hanks Center
1100 Pennsylvania Avenue, NW
Washington, DC 20506

Dear Patrice:

Enclosed please find the Katherine Dunham Center's application for continued NEA support as an Expansion Arts organization.

In addition to the required application form (one original and two copies), the supplementary information sheet (3 copies), the signed artistic statement (3 copies) and the IRS determination letter, we include two packets of materials. Each contains biographies of key artistic staff, a brief history of our organization, and materials on our three principal programs for FY90-91.

In particular, we are pleased with the greatly increased participation in the Dunham Technique Seminar; a full attendance and financial report, as well as sample brochure and schedule are included for the panel's review. I also enclose recent press coverage, which includes two articles on the Dunham Centers that appeared in the *New York Times*. We are very excited about receiving such unprecedented national attention, and grateful to the NEA for helping to make our growth possible.

As always, if you have a question about our application, please contact me at our St. Louis office, or Jeanelle Stovall at our East St. Louis number. The Katherine Dunham Centers thank the NEA for its past support, and look forward to another years of successful partnership.

Sincerely,

Margaret A. Elliott
Director of Development

71

OMB No. 3135-0048 Expires 5/31/94   37

Expansion Arts Program

Organization Grant Application Form NEA-3 (Rev.)

Submit the original and three copies of this form, together with other required materials to: Information Management Division/EXA, 8th floor, National Endowment for the Arts, Nancy Hanks Center, 1100 Pennsylvania Avenue, N.W., Washington, DC 20506

I. Applicant Organization (name address, zip)

Katherine Dunham Centers for Arts and Humanities
524 Trinity Avenue, Room 5
St. Louis, MO 63130-4314

III. Period of support requested:

Starting 10/ 01/ 92
    month day year

Ending 09/ 30/ 93
    month day year

IV. Employer I.D. Number: 237099934

II. Category under which support is requested:

☒ EXPANSION ARTS ORGANIZATIONS

☐ Performing Arts (Circle one item below)
  Dance Theater Music

☐ Visual, Media, or Design Arts (Circle one item below)
  Visual Arts Media Design Combination

☐ Literary Arts

☒ Multidisciplinary

☐ SERVICES TO THE FIELD
☐ SPECIAL PROJECTS (Circle one item below)
  Rural Arts Initiative Arts Education Initiative

V. Summary of project description (Complete in space provided. Please DO NOT use photoreduction to fit more words into this space.)

Support is requested to continue and expand the existing programs of the Katherine Dunham Centers for Arts and Humanities. The Dunham Centers are a nonprofit, multi-disciplinary arts organization founded by, and currently operated under the artistic direction and leadership of, dance legend Katherine Dunham. The organization exists to promote and preserve Dunham's legacy as embodied in her innovative dance training technique and choreography, as well as her anthropological writings, films, and works of visual art. The Centers operate the Katherine Dunham Dynamic Museum, urban East St. Louis's only cultural center. The Museum houses collections of African and Carribean folk and contemporary art, and an extensive body of material documenting Dunham's life and work. In addition, the Centers operate a professionally directed, year-round arts training program for urban children aged four to seventeen, and an annual two-week seminar in Dunham Technique that attracts dancers, choreographers and scholars from around the world. All three programs emphasize Dunham's unique concept of "humanization and socialization of individuals and communities through the arts."

VI. Estimated number of persons expected to benefit from this project	55,000

VII. Summary of estimated costs (recapitulation of budget items in Section X)

	Total costs of project
A. Direct costs	
Salaries and wages	$ 205,200
Fringe benefits	$ 22,000
Supplies and materials	$ 20,300
Travel	$ 61,180
Permanent equipment	$ 46,000
Fees and other	$ 142,950
Total direct costs	$ 497,630
B. Indirect costs	$ -0-
Total project costs	$ 497,600
(rounded to nearest $100)	

VIII. Total amount requested from the National Endowment for the Arts .... $ 90,000

NOTE: This amount (amount requested): $ 90,000
PLUS Total contributions, grants, and revenues (XI, page 3):   + 407,600
MUST EQUAL Total project costs (VII. above):   = 497,600

IX. Organization total fiscal activity

		1990-91 Actual			1991-92 Estimate
A. Expenses	1. $	255,716	2. $		343,250
B. Contributions, grants, & revenues	1. $	223,961	2. $		329,200

Type names requested below:
Authorizing Official: Dr. Cynthia W. Hardy   Project Director: Jeanelle Stovall

73

38

2

X. Budget breakdown of summary of estimated costs

A. Direct costs

1. Salaries and wages

Title and/or type of personnel	Number of personnel	Annual or average salary range	% of time devoted to this project	Amount $
Founder/International Artistic Director			.20	
Executive Director			.50	
Associate Director			.30	
Director of Development			1.00	
Assistant Artistic Director			1.00	
Children's Workshop Director			.50	
Ballet Mistress			.50	
Assistant Teachers (2)			.50	
Registrar/Curator			1.00	
AV Technician/Facilities Manager			.50	
Gallery Attendant			.50	
Secretary			1.00	
Office Assistant			.50	
				205,200

Fringes @ 15% for permanent staff only

Total salaries and wages	$ 205,200
Add fringe benefits	$ 22,000
Total salaries and wages including fringe benefits	$ 227,200

2. Supplies and materials (list each major type separately)

Amount
$

Brochures, Flyers, promotional materials – printing/postage	11,900
Workshop Costumes and supplies	2,000
Seminar class materials	1,400
Museum – docent training materials	3,000
Invitations for special events	2,000
Total supplies and materials $	20,300

3. Travel

a. Transportation of personnel

No. of travelers	from	to	Amount $
Children's Workshop Faculty (2) @ $600 average airfare			1,200
Dance Seminar Faculty (25) @ $300 average airfare			7,500
Misc. Travel – Museum guest lecturers, staff			12,000
		Total transportation of personnel $	20,700

b. Subsistence

No. of travelers	No. of days	Daily rate	Amount $
Children's Workshop Faculty (2), 28 days @ $80/day			4,480
Dance Seminar Faculty (25), 18 days @ $80/day			36,000
		Total subsistence $	40,480
		Total travel (a. + b.) $	61,180

X. Budget breakdown of summary of estimated costs (continued)

4. Permanent equipment

	Amount
	$
Audio-Visual Equipment & Supplies	30,000
15-passenger van	16,000
Total permanent equipment	$ 46,000

NOTE: Endowment funds are not sought for these items.

5. Fees for services and other expenses (list each item separately)

	Amount
	$
Security, Maintenance, Telephones, etc.	20,000
Honoraria – Workshop, Seminar Faculty; Museum Lecturers	57,500
Fees – Contract Teachers, Adult Classes	5,700
Seminar AV Technician and Equipment	6,250
Fees – Museum and Seminar Evaluators	8,000
Receptions, Seminar Meals	10,000
Seminar Space Rental	5,000
Insurance	15,000
Seminar and Workshop Utilities	2,500
Museum Utilities	10,000
Seminar Van Rentals	3,000
Total fees and other	$ 142,950

B. Indirect costs

	Amount
	$

Rate established by attached negotiation agreement with
National Endowment for the Arts or another Federal agency

Rate _____ % Base _____

$ ____N/A____

XI. Contributions, grants and revenues (for this project)

A. Contributions

1. Cash   **Amount**

$ _____

2. In-kind contributions (list each major item)

	Amount
Donated printing and Postage	3,000
Donated Workshop Costumes	500
In-Kind Van Rental	1,400
Donated Van	16,000
Donated AV Equipment	30,000
Total contributions	$ 50,900

B. Grants (do not list anticipated grant from the Arts Endowment)

Government Grants - Federal, State, Local	73,000
Corporate Contributions	41,000
Foundation Grants	95,000
Grants from Individuals	43,700
Total grants	$ 252,700

C. Revenues

Spring Fund-Raising Benefit	50,000
Fall Direct Mail Appeal	10,000
Seminar and Class Registrations	42,000
Seminar Boutique Sales	2,000
Total revenues	$ 104,000
Total contributions, grants, and revenue for this project	$ 407,600

Katherine Dunham Centers for Arts and Humanities

40

4

XII. Final Reports

Have you submitted required Final Report packages on all completed grants from any Arts Endowment Program since (and including) Fiscal Year 1984?

_____ Yes __X__ No   If no, and you have received Arts Endowment funding in the past, please mail immediately, under separate cover, to Grants Office/Final Reports Section to maintain eligibility. Do not include with your application package.   Final Report on FY91 Grant due 12/31/91.

XIII. Delinquent Debt

Are you delinquent on repayment of any Federal debt? _____ Yes __X__ No
If yes, provide explanatory information on a separate sheet.

XIV. Certification

The Authorizing Official(s) certify that the information contained in this application, including all attachments and supporting materials, is true and correct to the best of our knowledge. The Authorizing Official(s) also certify that the applicant will comply with the Federal requirements specified under "Assurance of Compliance" on pages 25-28.

Authorizing Official(s)

Signature   x _Cynthia W. Hardy_____ Date signed __10/09/91__
Name (print or type)   Dr. Cynthia W. Hardy
Title (print or type)   Executive Director
Telephone (area code)   314-863-0525

Signature   x _____ Date signed _____
Name (print or type)   _____
Title (print or type)   _____
Telephone (area code)   _____

Project director

Signature x _Jeanelle Stovall_ _____ Date signed 10/09/91

Name (print or type) Jeanelle Stovall

Title (print or type) Associate Director

Telephone (area code) 618-271-3367

Payee (to whom grant payments will be sent if other than authorizing official)

Signature x _____ Date signed _____

Name (print or type) _____

Title (print or type) _____

Telephone (area code) _____

*If payment is to be made to anyone other than the grantee, it is understood that the grantee is financially, administratively, and programmatically responsible for all aspects of the grant and that all reports must be submitted through the grantee.

BEFORE SEALING YOUR APPLICATION PACKAGE, BE SURE TO INCLUDE IN THE FOLLOWING ORDER:

☒ Application Acknowledgment Card
☒ Application form
☒ Supplementary Information Sheet
☒ IRS Letter
☒ Site Visit Card (Expansion Arts Organizations and Services to the Field applicants)

☒ For Expansion Arts Organizations applicants, artistic statement (three copies) and TWO SEPARATE SETS OF:
☒ Biographies of key staff
☒ History of organization
☒ Program documentation (Services to the Field applicants: note requirement for description of project plan on pages 31-32)

Check on pages 30-32 in the "How to Apply" Section for a list of all materials required for your project request. Applicants under Expansion Arts Organizations should also refer to "Special Requirements" on pages 13-14. Your application is incomplete without these materials and may be rejected.

Privacy Act

The Privacy Act of 1974 requires us to furnish you with the following information:

The Endowment is authorized to solicit the requested information by Section 5 of the National Foundation on the Arts and the Humanities Act of 1965, as amended. The information is used for grant processing, statistical research, analysis of trends, and for congressional oversight hearings. Failure to provide the requested information could result in rejection of your application.

79

OMB No. 3135-0048 Expires 5/31/94   41

Expansion Arts Supplementary Information Sheet

Please complete both sides of this form. Return three clear copies with your application package. Provide all information in the space provided.

Name of applicant: Katherine Dunham Centers for Arts and Humanities

Address: 524 Trinity Avenue
St. Louis, MO 63130-4314

Contact person: Margaret A. Elliott

Phone: 314-863-0525

1. Describe your organization in terms of: a) fundamental purpose; b) governance structure and staff; c) artists and art forms; d) audiences and/or recipients of services; and e) the culturally diverse, inner city, rural or tribal community served. Where appropriate, include racial/ethnic composition. Use only space provided.

The Katherine Dunham Centers were founded by Dunham in 1970 as the Dunham Fund for Research and Development of Cultural Arts. The organization focuses on new forms of education and human relations. Its fundamental purpose is to promote research and training in the arts and humanities, leading to 1) arts-based communication techniques for people of diverse cultures, and 2) a multi-arts training program to humanize and socialize individuals, as well as provide them with marketable skills. It achieves these ends through continued scholarship in the field of intercultural communication, carried on by Dunham and others, and an innovative arts training program developed and perfected by Dunham in the late 1960s. The Centers recently reorganized under a new name, and have taken important steps to ensure long-term survival and growth. These include formation of three groups to provide counsel and fund-raising assistance: a twenty-member Board of Directors, with representatives from East St. Louis and St. Louis; an International Advisory Board, comprised of arts leaders from around the country; and an Artistic Advisory Committee for the Seminar, peopled by leading scholars and dancers proficient in Dunham Technique. With grant support -- including NEA assistance --

(See reverse)

the Centers have hired a part-time professional administrator and a full-time development officer to augment a part-time professional artistic staff. The Dunham Centers include a network of outstanding visual and performing artists, educators, and researchers, who make available their knowledge and skills. The entire St. Louis metro area, particularly the East St. Louis community, benefits from the workshops, seminars, and performances given by Dunham Centers instructors, lecturers, and dancers. East St. Louis is an urban community of some 50,000 inhabitants, 98% of them black, with over 50% of the population receiving some form of Federal aid. While the artistic potential in East St. Louis is great (it was home to jazz legend Miles Davis, among others), the negative economic factors have traditionally eclipsed this aspect of society. The city operates without a single movie house or legitimate theatre. Cultural activites for young people do not exist. For this reason, the Dunham Centers place special emphasis on arts training for some fifty children between the ages of four and seventeen, including a select group being schooled in Dunham Technique. This core group of twenty youngsters, who currently demonstrate and perform Dunham Technique and choreography for area schools and community groups, will eventually qualify to teach.

81

42

Expansion Arts Supplementary Information Sheet (Continued)

2. Total budget for this project: $ 497,600   Amount requested from Expansion Arts: $ 90,000

3. Year organization was founded: 1970

4. Do you own your facility? X Yes _____ No. If yes, please describe (e.g., offices, performance/exhibition space):
Museum Building, Carriage House Dance Studio, Office/Residence Halls, Storage Building

5. Do you offer training programs? X Yes _____ No.

6. Please provide the following information on the organization's total fiscal activity for the most recently completed fiscal year.
NOTE: If your organization has an audit available for the most recently completed fiscal year, you are encouraged to submit a copy in addition to completing this form.

DATES OF FISCAL YEAR: from   01/01/90   to   12/31/90

EXPENSES

Salaries/fees

Artistic personnel	$ 42,000
Technical staff	7,800
Administrative	42,000
Subtotal, Salaries/fees	91,800

Program expenses

Productions	2,000
Exhibitions	3,000
Classes/workshops	10,000
Services	-0-
Other	110,500
Subtotal, Program expenses	125,500

INCOME

Earned Income

Box office	-0-
Contracts	-0-
Sales Seminar Fees	23,500
Other (describe) Admissions	500
Performance Fees	1,500
Subtotal, Earned Income	25,500

Contributed Income

Expansion Arts grant	
Other Arts Endowment	75,000

Marketing expenses — 3,000

Fundraising expenses — 1,500

Facilities expenses
Check: rent ☒ mortage ☒
In-kind ☐ other ☐ — 50,000

Other expenses (list)
Travel - Seminar — 45,000

TOTAL EXPENSES — 316,800

grants (list)
Expansion Arts: — 35,000
Development Staff

Other Federal funds (list) — -0- / -0-

State government sources — 11,200

Local government sources — 63,000

Individuals — 5,000

Corporations (total) Anheuser-Busch — 23,000
(attach list)

Foundations (total) LINKS — 35,000
(attach list) Ford

In-kind (total) Staff — 37,000
(attach list)

Subtotal, Contributed Income — 284,200

TOTAL INCOME — 309,700

SURPLUS OR (DEFICIT)

Fund balance beginning of year — 3,378.52
Fund balance end of year — -6,721.48
Net current assets (liabilities) end of year — 313,421.48

83

Brief Biographies of Key Artistic Staff

Katherine Dunham

Katherine Dunham....dancer, choreographer, actress, writer, producer, composer, educator, anthropologist....a remarkable woman....even in an era of remarkable women....Born in Chicago, Illinois, to Albert Millard Dunham and Fannie Guillaume Dunham, Katherine Dunham graduated from Joliet Township High School and Junior College. She received her bachelor's, master's (in anthropology) and doctoral (of philosophy) degrees from the University of Chicago, and has since been awarded eighteen Honorary Doctorates in Fine Arts, Humane Letters and Law.

Miss Dunham has achieved international fame and respect for her contribution to the performing arts. Her appearances in opera houses and open air theatres, in night clubs and hotels, in the movies and on television have taken her to all parts of the globe: North and South America, Europe, Australia and the Near and Far East.

Her film credits include appearances in the Hollywood productions ''Star Spangled Rhythm,'' ''Stormy Weather,'' ''Casbah,'' and ''Mambo.'' She has appeared in TV spectaculars for the BBC in London; National TV in Paris; CBS Toronto; American Spectacular; NBC Esso World Theatre, New York; and guested frequently on interview and panel shows.

Miss Dunham has been a guest lecturer at numerous universities, among them Yale University, the University of Chicago, Case-Western Reserve University, Stanford University, Harvard University, and Ohio State University in the United States; and the Royal Anthropological Society, Brussels and London. She continues to speak at colleges and universities throughout the world. A prolific writer of newspaper and magazine articles, she has also won a wide following for her excellent short stories and autobiographical works. A talented artist, Miss Dunham has exhibited her paintings in Paris, Milan, London, Sidney, Lima, and Buenos Aires.

Katherine Dunham has been honored for her contribution to the arts since 1937, when she was recognized by the Honorary Women's Scientific Fraternity of the University of Chicago. Her many awards include the Chevalier of Haitian Legion of Honor and Merit, 1952; Laureate and Member, Lincoln Academy, 1968; Dance Magazine Award, 1969; Certificate of Merit, International Who's Who in Poetry, 1971; Contribution to the Arts Award, Black Academy of Arts and Letters, 1972; National Center of Afro-American Artists Award, Elma Lewis School of Fine Arts; Black Merita Academy Award, 1972; Albert Schweitzer Award, 1979; the Grande Croix of The Haitian Legion of Honor and Merit; the Kennedy Center Honors, 1983; the American Dance Festival Award, 1986; the President's National

Medal of the Arts, 1988; Essence Magazine's Essence Award, 1990; the NAACP-Hollywood Chapter's Image Awards Hall of Fame, 1990; and St. Louis University's Sword of Ignatius Loyola, 1991.

After a long and distinguished teaching career with the campuses of Southern Illinois University, where she founded a Performing Arts Training Center that still bears her name, Miss Dunham retired and became University Professor Emerita at S.I.U. - Edwardsville. She presently serves as Founder and International Artistic Director for the Katherine Dunham Centers for Arts and Humanities in East St. Louis, dividing her time between the programs of the Centers and her own projects in Haiti.

Master Instructors

Yanoye Aikens was a leading man with the Dunham Company for many years, appearing with Dunham in ''Tropical Revue,'' ''Ballet Negre,'' ''Concert Varieties,'' ''Carib Song,'' ''Bamboche,'' and in many nightclubs. He is the former head of the Jazz Department at Danshogskoian, the Dance Larare of Jazz at Knuglia Opera in Stockholm, Sweden. Mr. Aikens has also been a guest Professor of Dance at the Department of Education Physique in Brussels and Brugge, Belgium; at Ann Malares Escuela in Barcelona; and at the University of Maryland for three seasons. Now relocated to Southern California, Mr. Aikens guest teaches at Cal Ars, Santa Monica City College, and Glendale City College. He recently completed a video-documentary of his teaching methods in Sweden.

Talley Beatty was one of the original members of the Dunham Company when it formed in 1940. In 1945, he danced in New York for the film, ''Study in Choreography for Camera,'' a composition by Maya Deren. Mr. Beatty also appeared in several major productions as the leading male dancer, including ''Showboat,'' ''Spring in Brazil,'' and ''Black Face.'' In 1959, Mr. Beatty made his first major contribution to the dance world as a leading choreographer for ''The Road of Phoebe Snow,'' He has continued his work as a significant African-American choreographer, using movement styles, music, and idioms unique to African-American culture. In a recent season, the Alvin Ailey Company paid tribute to Mr. Beatty with a full evening performance of his work.

Lucille Ellis was discovered by Katherine Dunham in Chicago, where Ms. Ellis received her basic training in classic, tap, swing, and Dunham techniques. Ms. Ellis toured as a featured dancer with the Dunham Company, and now serves as liaison between past and present Dunham Technique dancers. She has been a sustaining member of the Seminar faculty, helping to train students and future teachers. In addition to her work with the Dunham Company, Ms. Ellis danced with the American Ballet Theatre and the Agnes de Mille Heritage Dance Theatre. She is an Affiliate Artist.

Tommy Gomez was also one of the founding and original members of the Dunham Company. He is presently an instructor of Dunham Technique at the Richard Daly and Kennedy King City College of Chicago, Illinois. Mr. Gomez has performed extensively on Broadway, and on Chicago stages. He appeared in ''Cabin in the Sky,'' ''Carib Song,'' ''Show Boat,'' ''Concert Varieties,'' ''The King and I,'' and ''Beggars' Holiday.'' His film credits include appearances in such Hollywood productions as ''Star-Spangled Rhythm,'' ''Stormy Weather,'' ''Casbah,'' and ''Mambo.'' Mr. Gomez was a member of Dunham's faculty from 1969-1976, when she headed the Performing Arts Training Center at Southern Illinois University-East St. Louis. During his tenure, he taught primitive rhythms and Dunham Technique. He also served as coordinator, registrar, and student counselor for the PATC's performing company. From 1977-79, Mr. Gomez coordinated the Dance Touring Program of the Illinois Arts Council. Between 1981-83, he also directed a dance program for the hearing impaired for the Chicago Council on Fine Arts. Mr. Gomez is a recipient of the Thelma Hill Dance Award for Outstanding Contribution to Dance by a Male Dancer, and the Ruth Paige Award.

Guest Instructors

Doris Bennett-Glasper is a graduate of Southern Illinois University at Edwardsville. She was a dancer with the Performing Arts Training Center founded by Dunham, where she not only toured with the company but also taught beginning Dunham Technique and gave classes for area community centers and schools. Ms. Bennett-Glasper divides her time between the United States and Rome, Italy, where she has performed in films and on television, and worked as a professional model.

Cornelius Kweku Ganyo, known affectionately as ''Uncle C.K.,'' has been teaching West African music and dance at Cal Arts for the past year, in conjunction with Kobla LadZeekpo. As head of the National Folkloric Company of the Arts Council of Ghana from 1966-83, Mr. Ganyo travelled throughout Ghana to research new material for the ethnic groups: Ashanti, Dagbani, Fanti, Ga, etc. As a member of many Ghanaian cultural tours, he has performed throughout Africa, Eastern and Western Europe, India, Israel, Singapore, and the United States. He has written and directed many West African dance dramas: <u>Tears for a Stranger</u>, <u>Ode to</u>

Osaquefo -- and recorded <u>Seventeen Ghanaian Traditional Musics</u> with the National Folkloric Company and Edinkafo Dance Band. Mr. Ganyo was also involved in Mick Fleetwood's recording, <u>The Visitor</u>. He served as Artistic Director of the Children's Dance Theatre of Ghana during its residence at Community Drum, Nashville, TN in 1983. The company performed in many major cities, including an appearance at the New Orleans World's Fair in 1984.

Lusiness Luisnes, a former member of the National Ballet of Haiti, is a long-time friend and associate of Jean-Leon Destine, a famous Haitian dancer. Mr. Luisnes is presently working in New York with dancers and performers of Haitian folklore.

Ronald Marshall, a dancer, actor and teacher of West African culture and theatre, first studied dance with his aunt, Sadie Bruce. He was introduced to Dunham Technique by Lucille Ellis, and through her training and guidance, came to study at Dunham's Performing Arts Training Center at SIU. With this background, he was accepted at the University of Ghana, finishing his undergraduate degree in African Studies with an emphasis on dance and drama. He has been active in theatre, on television, and in films, performing his own one-man show. In addition, Mr. Marshall is completing his Master's Thesis in Dance Ethnology at UCLA.

Alicia Pierce began formal dance training in rhythm, tap, ballet, acrobatics, and interpretive dance in 1956 at age five, in her hometown of New Orleans, Louisiana. She continued her training as a dance major at San Francisco State University. Ms. Pierce received her B.A. in Physical Education, with dance emphasis and a minor in Black Studies, in 1974. She became a member of the SFSU faculty, and continued her studies in Dunham Technique, Jazz, Modern, Primitive Rhythms, and Jazz Dance History in the Oakland/San Francisco Bay Area. As a member of the Wajumbe Cultural Ensemble from 1970-83, Ms. Pierce performed throughout the Bay Area, as well as in other parts of Southern California, and eventually Nevada, Texas, Ohio, and Lagos, Nigeria, at the Second World Festival of Black and African Arts and Culture. She has taught Master Classes in recreational centers, universities, junior colleges, and high schools. In 1990, she received an M.A. in Creative Arts, Interdisciplinary Studies.

Dr. Albirda Rose-Eberhardt received her Ed.D. in 1982, and is currently a full Professor of Dance at San Francisco State University. She is the author of Dunham Technique: A Way of Life. An accomplished dancer and choreographer, Dr. Rose also trained and performed professionally as a dramatic and vocal artist. While on sabbatical in 1986, she travelled with Dunham to Brazil to serve as a demonstrator and assistant. When not providing instruction in dance theory at San Francisco

State, she serves as founding coordinator and faculty member for the Dunham Technique Seminar. Dr. Rose heads the newly-formed Artistic Advisory Committee for the Seminar; she is a co-author and leading proponent of the proposed written certification guidelines for teachers of Dunham Technique.

Joe Sircus, percussionist and accompanist for many performing groups and schools in New York, directed his own Cuban folklore group. In 1989, he performed with and accompanied the Alvin Ailey Gala Performance, the "Magic of Katherine Dunham." Recently, he performed at the Dunham Centers' cabaret, "La Fete aux Antilles."

Kelvin Strong, a student of Lucille Ellis, met Miss Dunham during a lecture-demonstration at his high school in Chicago. There, he was director of the dance group, "Walla Wa Bascis." Not long after their meeting, he and his company came to the Performing Arts Training Center for a summer residency, where they trained with Master Instructors in dance, music, and drama. Mr. Strong has continued his work in percussion, becoming extremely proficient in Caribbean and African rhythms.

Rachel Jean-Louis Tavernier, a native of Haiti, began formal dance training at age five with Lavinia Williams. Her background is in ballet, jazz, primitive dance, and Dunham Technique. She owned and directed her own dance school in Haiti for over ten years. Most recently, Ms. Tavernier has performed with the GEMINI Dance Theatre in Buffalo, NY. She appeared in a Gala Tribute to Katherine Dunham, and was chosen by the American Dance Festival 1988 to attend a program for international choreographers. Ms. Tavernier has attended the Dunham Technique Seminar since its inception, and has worked as a demonstrator. She has also guest taught at the Children's Workshop.

Mor Thiam, a former Master Percussionist with the National Ballet of Senegal, joined Miss Dunham in 1968 to teach at the PATC. Since that time, he founded and directed the "Cosaan African Dance Company," a percussion group called "Drums of Fire," and the annual Drum and Dance Conference. He is presently Director of Les Ballets Africans, in residence at EPCOT Center, Disneyworld, Orlando, Florida.

Dr. Glory Van Scott -- actress, dancer, singer, writer, and producer of the Katherine Dunham Gala in 1979 -- comes from Chicago, where she studied dance with Edna Sommerville Oats at the Abraham Lincoln Center. Dr. Van Scott graduated from Goddard College in Vermont (B.A., M.A.), and received her Ph.D. in Education and Theatre Arts from the Union Graduate School in Ohio. Dr. Van

Scott also received an Eleanor Roosevelt NARIO in Human Relations, and was a Bread Loaf Writer's Scholar. She is an Affiliate Artist, having been a member of the Dunham Company, American Ballet Theatre, and the Agnes de Mille Heritage dance theatre.

Staff

Darryl Braddix is the Director of the Katherine Dunham Children's Workshop. His association with Miss Dunham began in 1967, when he was a member of an East St. Louis youth gang known as the Imperial Warlords. Mr. Bradddix didn't know it at the time, but soon after he met Miss Dunham, she began grooming him for his current responsibilities. As one of the primary Dunham Technique instructors for children, Mr. Braddix defines Dunham's work as a style of dance and a philosophy of life. His skills as a choreographer are in demand. In 1985, he choreographed the theatre production ''The Mighty Gents,'' for the Repertory Theatre of St. Louis. Recently, he performed in Los Angeles for a Gala Banquet hosted by Honda Motors Corporation. As Workshop Director, he regularly rehearses students and accompanies them to performances for school and community groups.

Robert Lee started his career with Dunham at the Performintg Arts Training Center in 1969, when he was still a Seargent in the Air Force. His interest in audio-visual work led to his becoming the PATC's Audio-Visual Technician, responsible for recording all classes, rehearsals and performances on videotape. He served as AV Technician for the Drum and Dance Conference, and as Stage Manager for the PATC Dance Company. Since leaving SIU in 1983, Mr. Lee has continued with Dunham as Audio-Visual Technician for the Dunham Centers, and on-site coordinator for the annual Dunham Technique Seminar.

Jeanelle Stovall currently serves as a special assistant to Miss Dunham and the volunteer Associate Director of the Dunham Centers, after nearly a decade as Executive Director. Ms. Stovall received her B.A. from Spelman College and three Certificates of Languages from the University of Grenoble. Ms. Stovall, who speaks five languages, met Miss Dunham in 1966 in Senegal and became her personal translator. In 1968, Ms. Stovall joined Dunham in East St. Louis as her assistant, and since that time has committed her life to Dunham's vision.

Brief History of
The Katherine Dunham Centers
for Arts and Humanities

The Katherine Dunham Centers for Arts and Humanities were founded by Katherine Dunham in 1969 and incorporated in 1970 as the Dunham Fund for Research and Development of Cultural Arts. The Center reorganized under their present name in 1991. The Dunham Centers were created ''for the educational, civic, social, and literary betterment of all persons.''

> Through the arts, the Dunham Centers seek to achieve the ''humanization and socialization of the individual and of the community as a whole,... guiding and encouraging people toward a fuller awareness of themselves and their potential cultural contributions to society, while enabling them to develop a greater understanding of the cultural dynamics of others.''

Dunham began her work in East St. Louis as a member of the faculty of Southern Illinois University. She was brought to the University in the late 1960s to found a Performing Arts Training Center, and create a curriculum in dance anthropology, a field she invented. The Dunham Centers were created to preserve and promote Dunham's art and scholarship, during and following her service to SIU. Upon Dunham's retirement from the University in 1981, the program she directed there was largely phased out, except for the training center that still bears her name. Individual elements were carried on by the Dunham Centers independent of the University, thanks to the extraordinary determination of Dunham and her staff. Today, the Dunham Centers are a cultural focal point for urban East St. Louis, and the St. Louis metropolitan region's only multi-disciplinary arts organization devoted to works from diverse cultures. The Dunham Centers operate three principal programs:

The **Katherine Dunham Dynamic Museum**. This ''living'' Museum of objects from many cultures was founded in 1967 by Dunham and her designer-husband, the late John Pratt. The Museum houses a wealth of material on their lives and achievements, including papers, films, videotapes, and works of art. It moved to its present location in the historic Judge Maurice Joyce home in 1977. African and Caribbean folk and contemporary art, performing costumes from the Dunham Company, original paintings by Dunham, and musical instruments are some of the collections on view in the Museum's five galleries. Tours are by appointment; admission is free.

The **Katherine Dunham Children's Workshop**. Begun in 1982, this comprehensive program of year-round dance training and art education for area youngsters employs an innovative, multi-disciplinary approach to cultural understanding. Students aged four to seventeen learn music, French, and visual arts techniques in addition to ballet, tap, jazz, modern, and Dunham dance techniques. The Workshop, held three times per week on average, is free to its fifty participants.

The **Institute for Intercultural Communication** began as a body of Scholars and programs dedicated to preserving and perpetuating the philosophical and scholarly underpinnings of Dunham's contribution to dance, as well as her physical technique and choreograpy. It sponsored the first international **Dunham Technique Seminar** in 1984. The Seminar, now entering its ninth year, is a prestigious annual gathering of students, scholars and professionals from sixteen states and ten foreign countries. Participants -- about 175 in 1991 -- come to St. Louis for two weeks each summer to study with Dunham, former members of the Dunham Company, and other music and dance professionals. Tuition is modest ($475 per adult for 78 classes), with daily and single class rates available. Special sessions in primitive rhythms and theatre are tailored to students twelve and under.

Despite years of financial hardship and a dwindling staff, Dunham's monumental legacy has been preserved in the three programs noted above. Thanks to extraordinary financial and technical support from the National Endowment for the Arts, the State of Illinois, and the Ford Foundation, the Dunham Centers are putting new structures and personnel in place, to ensure continued survival of these programs.

1991 KATHERINE DUNHAM TECHNIQUE SEMINAR

SUMMARY PROGRAM REPORT

SEMINAR PARTICIPATION

By Category:	Adults	Children
Paid Registrants		
Full Seminar	8	3
Week One or Week Two Only	10	1
Single Day or Block of Six	16	0
Single Classes	45	6
Total Paid	79	10
	Adults	Children
Subsidized Registrants		
Scholarship	1	25
Work-Study:		
Full Tuition Waiver	2	7
Partial Tuition Waiver	2	1
Complimentary (Press, etc.):		
Full Seminar	3	0
Single Day	4	0
Single Class	7	0
Total Subsidized	19	33
Additonal Participants		
Master Instructors	5	

Instructors	6
Accompanists	7
Technical Staff	4
Volunteers and Special Guests	14
Total Additional Participants	36

By Geographic Area:

East Coast	West Coast	Midwest	South	Foreign
17	6	6	132	5	17

TOTAL 1991 SEMINAR PARTICIPATION   177

SUMMARY FINANCIAL REPORT

SEMINAR EXPENSES

Personnel

Artist's Fee – Founder	$2,500
Faculty Honoraria	$16,000

Artists' Travel	$5,000
Hotel/Housing	$7,900
Per Diem	$6,400
AV Technician	$1,200
Drivers	$1,000
Documentary Producer	$2,400
Total Personnel	$42,400
Seminar Operating Expenses	
Space Rental, COCA	$3,700
AV Equipment/Supplies	$4,500
Design Fees – Brochure	$500
Printing, 3 Flyers + Postcard	$2,800
Postage, Flyers	$750
Copying/Faxing	$1,400
Communications	$500
Van Rental	$3,900
Food/Reception	$100
T-Shirts/Books	$2,000
Total Operating Expenses	$20,150
Scholarship Expense (Revenue Forgone)	$9,869
TOTAL SEMINAR EXPENSES	$72,419
SEMINAR REVENUES	

Sponsorship Support	
NEA Operating Grant Allocation	$25,000
Illinois Arts Council Grant Allocation	$2,500
Anheuser-Busch Grant	$3,500
AT&T Grant	$2,500
CALOP Grant for Seminar Documentary	$10,000
East St. Louis Schools – Contribution	$375
Essence Communications – Contribution	$100
Dr. Albirda Rose-Eberhardt – Contribution	$40
Total Cash Revenues	$44,015
In-Kind Assistance	
AT&T – Printing and Postage, Main Brochure	$3,000
AT&T – Donated Van and Driver	$1,400
M. C. Dunham-Pratt – Computer Supplies	$40
Elliott Family – Seminar Housing	$200
Parker Group – Creative Services for Brochure	$500
Sutherland Home Supply – Lumber for Stage	$800
Tusten Townhomes – Instructor Housing	$500

	Number	Amount
Work-Study Contributions		$3,456
Total In-Kind Revenues		$9,856
Class Sales		
Adult Full Weeks @ $237.50	28	$6,650
Child Full Weeks @ $118.75	7	$831
Single Days/Blocks @ $50.00	35	$1,750
Adult Single Classes @ $15.00	116	$1,740
Child Single Classes @ $7.50	6	$45
Additonal Deposit Income		$225
Total Class Sales		$11,241
Merchandise/Misc. Sales		
Books and Souvenier Posters		$417
Seminar T-Shirts		$660
Bus Tickets		$85
Total Merchandise/Misc. Sales		$1,162
TOTAL SEMINAR REVENUES		$66,274
SEMINAR OPERATING DEFICIT		($6,145)

Success with the Ford Foundation:
United Way Sustains Support for Housing Initiative

The Institution: United Way of America (UWA) is a national service organization assisting its members in providing fundraising and social planning to help meet the nation's social welfare needs. The United Way system, comprised of more than 2,100 autonomous local United Ways, raises funds, provides technical assistance, planning, management and organizational support to more than 44,000 nonprofit agencies throughout the United States. In 1991, the United Way system raised over $3.1 billion, making it the largest private funder of services in the nation and second only to the Federal Government overall. United Ways also have considerable experience working collaboratively with other community stakeholders to identify critical issues in their community and then convene broad-based, highly visible public/private partnerships to develop innovative community initiatives that address the identified needs. Affordable housing is one of these issues.

The Author: Ellen Gilligan, Director of the Housing Initiative Program, is the author of the 1990 proposal to the Ford Foundation. Ms. Gilligan began her tenure as the Director of the Housing Initiative Program in 1988. Prior to joining the UWA staff, Ms. Gilligan worked as Deputy Project Director for the Local Initiatives Support Corporation (LISC), where she managed and provided direct technical assistance on management, real estate and business development issues to over 75 community-based development organizations, managed a $1.1 million portfolio, and assisted in the management of loan and grant portfolios totalling $3 million.

Background: The $760,000 Ford Foundation grant awarded to UWA in 1990 represents phase 2 of a $1.5 million Ford Foundation grant awarded to UWA in October 1987, which created the UWA Housing Initiative Program. Ford's interest in supporting UWA's efforts to start a national housing initiative stemmed from the success of the United Way of the Massachusetts Bay's (UWMB's) Neighborhood Development Support Collaborative. The Collaborative is currently providing operational support to 13 community development corporations (CDCs) which have restored or created some 3,000 units of housing and have 1,200 units under construction with another 300 units in planning. Based on the Collaborative's success, the Ford Foundation recognized untapped potential in the United Way system to support CDCs and local housing and community development efforts nationwide. Moreover, Ford viewed UWA as the catalyst to maximize that potential. Therefore, in October 1987, the Ford Foundation awarded UWA a two year, $1.5 million grant.

February 22, 1990

Ms. Nancy O. Andrews
Program Officer
Urban Poverty Program
320 East 43rd Street
New York, NY 10017

Dear Nancy:

United Way of America is requesting $760,000 over two years to support ongoing monitoring, technical assistance, and evaluation of the current Housing Initiatives Program; and to undertake specific information sharing, training and technical assistance activities aimed at increasing a dramatically greater number of United Way's capacity and expanding their involvement in addressing the affordable housing problems in their communities, specifically in support of community development corporations.

As you know, United Way of America has a current Ford Foundation grant which supports its Housing Initiatives Program. That grant is scheduled to expire at the end of February. Therefore, in order to prevent any interruption of program activities, we propose that the new grant term be for two years, beginning April 1, 1990.

We hope that this proposal is satisfactory. While it may be slightly longer than anticipated, the first ten pages are provided for you as background information, in an effort to give you a better working knowledge of the project, since you were not involved from the outset.

We appreciate your interest and support and look forward to working with you.

Sincerely,

Thomas M. Nunan
Vice President
Community Initiatives

cc: Ellen Gilligan

An Initiative to Expand and Institutionalize United Way Capacity to Address Affordable Housing Problems

A Proposal to the Ford Foundation

I. BACKGROUND

In September 1987, United Way of America received a grant of $1,500,000 from the Ford Foundation to undertake a national demonstration program intended to expand the involvement of local United Ways in addressing the housing needs of low- and moderate-income persons in their communities and two related projects aimed at strengthening fundraising capacity of local United Ways.

In the housing component, $750,000 was used by United Way of America to provide challenge grants and technical assistance in five localities to help them establish funding partnerships to support low-income housing activities of community development corporations (CDCs). ($500,000 was used to provide challenge grants; $250,000 provided staffing, technical sssistance and overhead support for a two and one half year period.)

The five city demonstration was modeled after a United Way effort in Boston -- the Neighborhood Development Support Collaborative -- where the United Way of Massachusetts Bay joined the Ford Foundation and other local foundations and the Local Initiatives Support Corporation (LISC) to assemble a $4.45 million pool of funds to be used to provide operating support to 10 CDCs over a five-year period. Of this amount, the United Way of Massachusetts Bay is contributing $1.8 million.

The provision of multi-year operating support is expected to help CDCs expand their production of lower income housing and economic development projects, and at the same time, increase their capacity to maintain organizationally, fiscally, and programmatically sound operations with long term stability. Like the Boston program, the national demonstration program is aimed at accomplishing the following goals:

o   Increasing the capacity of CDCs with respect to their housing production and organizational development;

o   Expanding the involvement of United Ways in addressing the affordable housing problems in their communities;

o   Through the leadership of United Ways, attracting new funders to local housing and economic development efforts; and, o Establishing a set of precedents for the ultimate affiliation of CDCs with United Way.

Although the programs established through the national demonstration vary in each location, a basic requirement is for United Ways to bring together philanthropies, business, and state and local governments to establish a pool of resources to provide operating support, training, and technical assistance to CDCs over a multi-year period.

II. SELECTION PROCESS

The program was designed as a challenge grant program in which United Way of America selected five local United Ways (or consortia of United Ways representing neighboring communities) for participation in the demonstration program through a two-stage Request for Proposal (RFP) process. The highlights of that process are as follows:

o Over 100 United Ways responded to the initial announcement of the Request for Proposals (RFP).

o A two-day Project Orientation Conference was held in Boston February 16-17, 1988 and was attended by 64 representatives of local United Ways.

o The first stage RFP required local United Ways to conduct an initial assessment of the needs and resources in their communities and to describe on a preliminary basis the proposed structure of a program that would meet those needs.

    Twenty-eight preliminary proposals were received by United Way of America on June 1, 1988.

o An initial review process was conducted by a team of reviewers consisting of project staff, United Way of America personnel, national housing technicians and consultants, and CDC directors from non-competitive cities. A National Advisory Committee, chaired by Larry D. Horner, Chairman and CEO of Peat Marwick Main and Co. and comprised of national housing technicians and funders was formulated to oversee the project (see attached). The Committee selected 11 finalist communities in July 1988.

o A second round RFP was distributed to the finalist communities in August, and project staff made two-day site visits to all finalist communities.

o The National Advisory Committee met in November 1988 and selected the following grantee communities: Chicago, IL; Houston, TX; Pontiac, MI; Rochester, NY; and York County, PA. Initial grant payments were made in January 1989.

In selecting the United Ways to participate in the demonstration program, United Way of America used the following criteria:

a. Commitment of the local United Way to address the housing needs of its community;

b. The willingness of the local United Way to make a financial commitment to the program;

c. Willingness and demonstrated ability of the local United Way to broker relationships among the philanthropic, corporate, business and labor communities, state and local government officials, CDCs, housing advocates and social service providers to generate financial and political support for the program;

d. The presence of a sufficient number of CDCs with demonstrated capacity to develop affordable housing;

e. The adequacy of the local housing delivery system -- i.e., the accessibility and availability of sufficient project financing, technical assistance and other resources -- to support expanded housing development efforts;

f. A willingness to consider CDCs eligible for affiliation with the United Way on an ongoing basis;

g. The availability of training and technical assistance providers;

h. Demonstrated commitment and capacity to operate the program (e.g., volunteers, staff, and plans in place); and

i. The adequacy of the proposed program in light of the scale, needs and resources of the local community.

III.   PROGRAM STATUS AND LESSONS LEARNED

Three-year, $100,000 grants were awarded in January 1989. In most sites, start-up activities took several months, so CDCs are just beginning to receive

United Way funds. It is premature at this time to assess program impact, but there are some particular strengths and weaknesses in each program site and a number of general lessons learned which are of interest.

A. SITE SPECIFIC STRENGTHS AND WEAKNESSES

o   Chicago has made the most significant financial and institutional commitment to the program, and to ongoing support for CDCs. United Way of Chicago has committed nearly $5 million over an eight-year period, through a total restructuring of its allocations process. Thirty-five CDCs will receive assistance, and 15 to 20 CDCs will be admitted as member agencies during that period of time. Housing has been identified as a priority area for United Way of Chicago, and its Board is committed to this restructuring and support of CDCs. United Way of Chicago is working very closely with LISC and its MacArthur Foundation-supported Fund for Community Development.

   The emergence of United Way in this area represents significant new resources supporting CDCs in Chicago, and a major shift in priorities for the United Way. Due to extensive structural and programmatic changes required, including revising membership standards to take into account the special needs of CDCs, eligibility for membership will not be available to CDCs until July 1990. However, United Way of Chicago has allocated nearly $181,000 in venture grants for such housing related programs as tenant organizing, emergency shelter, and housing development technical assistance and advocacy. While the $100,000 challenge grant was not the deciding factor in United Way of Chicago's move into this area, it did provide the administrative support to speed up the process, and the national demonstration helped legitimize and support structural changes for the Board of Directors.

   The Chicago program also includes a significant training and management assistance component, in addition to the training provided through the Fund for Community Development. Further, eligibility for United Way funding is not limited to those groups included in the Fund for Community Development. For a variety of reasons, including the development capacity of Chicago CDCs and the significant institutional change and commitment of the United Way of Chicago, this is the flagship of the demonstration program.

o   Houston currently has an undeveloped and inadequate housing delivery system. There are three CDCs that have some, though minimal, track record and LISC is undertaking an effort to organize and support new groups. That fact was acknowledged by the National Advisory Committee in selecting Houston to be part of the demonstration. LISC has made a significant technical and financial investment in Houston and it appears that the public and private sector banking community are slowly beginning to recognize and support CDCs. United Way support adds considerable legitimacy to this effort and broadens the base of private sector support. The United Way views this as a demonstration project. Long term commitment to support CDCs will be based on successes during this initial three-year period. The United Way in Houston has had considerable involvement in addressing homelessness in the community, and there is hope that if the CDCs can begin to produce, long term support for CDCs will be a natural extension of that effort. Houston is a challenging site for a number of reasons. First, because the infrastructure to support expanded housing development is underdeveloped. Second, this is the only demonstration site where the United Way did not hire a project coordinator. Although LISC provides substantial technical assistance, it is long distance, and there is little local technical assistance to provide day to day support. Finally, it is unclear how substantial Board level support is within United Way. United Way has agreed to hire project staff in the second year, and will work to increase Board level support in the coming months. Houston United Way is also undergoing a change in Executives, so it is unclear what impact this will have on the program. Much of the long term impact in Houston will depend on the initial visible successes of the CDCs.

o   Pontiac was rated highest overall in its initial program proposal, yet it has the least capacity in terms of community development of the demonstration sites. It is a community of considerable need, which has been hard hit by the downturn in the auto industry, and it is surrounded by communities of tremendous wealth. The United Way in Pontiac, though relatively small, has taken a real leadership position in addressing this issue. It has been quite successful in identifying and securing new sources of funds, and in providing a forum to highlight the housing needs in the community. There is a tremendous void in leadership among the public and private sector in terms of community development in Pontiac, and United Way has effectively stepped into a coordinating position.

There is only one active CDC, Pontiac NHS, and it has had some recent staff turnover. However, LISC has made Pontiac part of its nine-city Mott Foundation-supported program aimed at initiating local LISC programs. Activities in the coming months will focus on building the capacity of some neighborhood organizations to do development, and on stabilizing the NHS. LISC is using the example of the United Way program in Pontiac to promote United Way involvement in some of the other cities in Michigan. This program has had considerable impact on the United Way in Pontiac, which can hopefully be translated into broader community-wide impact, but building development capacity will be a long-term effort, given the current status. Long-term United Way support will most likely be dependent on the ability to get some housing development of scale underway.

o   Rochester is the only demonstration site which involves a consortia of six United Ways. United Way of Greater Rochester is the driving force, and has been involved in supporting housing development since 1968. However, there is a need to look at the housing needs in that area in regional terms, which includes the City of Rochester and the surrounding rural area. The surrounding areawide United Ways are small, largely volunteer organizations (i.e., without professional staff), and there is considerable work to be done in educating the Boards about housing needs and the role of CDCs. Rochester is the only site where LISC or the Enterprise Foundation is not involved, but there are a number of sophisticated CDCs which can and have provided technical assistance to smaller organizations in the past. The Rochester program is designed to formalize that process, while enabling the larger CDCs to expand their own development capacity. The city has a capable technical assistance staff, but only works with organizations inside the city limits. The city also has been in control of the community development efforts to date, and while it actively supports and participates in the United Way collaborative, there seems to be a power struggle going on about who will control and influence what goes on in the city. The outlying areas are free of these political struggles and there are a number of very good CDCs, and adequate project financing available through the state, so that may be the area where this effort has the greatest impact on development, despite the lack of sophistication of the smaller United Ways. Rochester is committed to this effort for five years, and their program plan calls for continued support for CDCs beyond that.

o   York County is the best example of a true collaborative at work. That is in part due to the size of the community, and the fact that the need, while significant, is not overwhelming. York's program has really taken hold. The United Way has made its Housing Initiatives Program its showcase effort in the community, and has been very successful in getting very broadbased support and participation in the program. The Advisory Committee is very active and committed, and is chaired by the President of the largest savings and loan association in the area. The Community Development Director for the City of York is the past Chairman of the United Way, and sits on the Committee, and the County Community Development Director is also actively involved. There is also strong, broadbased private sector support and participation. York has received statewide recognition for this program from the American Planning Association and the Governor and state legislature. After testimony by the Chair of the Housing Advisory Committee and the Enterprise Foundation, legislation is being introduced using the York Program as a model for statewide replication.

The Committee has taken on a strong advocacy and public policy role. Prior to United Way's involvement, the Enterprise Foundation had been working in York with one CDC. Their contract has been expanded to include the three groups which are developing projects, and one Housing Counseling Agency which administers a first-time homebuyer program for low- and moderate-income families. United Way of York has hired an experienced Housing Coordinator as project staff. One CDC selected for this program, which had not developed any new projects in several years, but had in the past developed several hundred units, currently has 110 units in various stages of pre-development. In terms of impact on development to date, York has achieved the most. The United Way is committed to this effort for at least five years, and there is every indication that CDCs will receive ongoing United Way support.

B. LESSONS LEARNED

o United Way Can Effectively Act as a Neutral Convenor and as a Catalyst to Broaden Support for Housing Activities and for CDCs.

United Ways are not seen as major stakeholders in the area of low-income housing development, and can act as a neutral convenor on the local level. United Ways have been able, at least initially, to de-politicize the process of collaboration and garner broadbased public and private sector support and participation. United Ways have also been viewed as bringing added value; the anticipation of additional resources commands a certain amount of attention and cooperation.

o United Ways Can Identify and Secure New Resources to Support These Efforts.

While it can be argued that some of the resources leveraged in the initial demonstration sites are not actually new additional resources, in all cases the collaborative effort of targeting local resources for capacity building, technical assistance, and operating support has added real value and given recognition to the need for ongoing operating support. In addition, United Ways have, in some cases, increased support for project financing and have in fact, secured significant new resources for operating support in all sites. This project has involved over 30 local funding partners in the five demonstration sites. In all cases, United Ways' collaborative efforts have broadened the base of involvement among the public and private sectors, in addition to increasing their own involvement.

o   The Presence of a National Technical and Financial Intermediary Enhances and Facilitates Development Impact But May Limit Ongoing United Way Involvement.

While the presence of LISC or the Enterprise Foundation in a demonstration site contributes significantly to the local technical capacity and the increased development capacity of CDCs, their presence makes it more difficult to evaluate the impact of United Way involvement. It is very difficult to evaluate the impact of operating support and technical assistance on increased production of housing units, especially given the presence of national intermediaries which have the goal of increased production as their primary mission. It will be very important in these demonstration sites that the added value of United Way's involvement be clearly documented, articulated, and recognized, in order that United Ways see it in their interest to provide ongoing support. This will be done through the volunteer committee, lessons and learnings and the final report.

o   In Order to Increase Technical Capacity and Achieve Institutional Change Within a United Way, There Must Be Strong Board Support and Commitment of Resources to the Issue.

As in a lot of organizations, the commitment to institutional change is directly related to the level of Board support and involvement and to the technical and financial resources dedicated to the effort. As seen in the demonstration sites, this factor is not necessarily related to the size of the community. For example, Chicago has tremendous resources to dedicate to this effort and is committed to doing so. York County and Pontiac, though considerably smaller, have committed proportionally significant resources. Houston, on the other hand, has not committed significant staff or financial resources, but we are hopeful that this will work out in the long-term, given growing local momentum, and we are certain to learn some different kinds of lessons from this site.

o   United Ways Can and Do Play a Variety of Roles in Addressing These Issues.

The mix of cities selected for this demonstration is representative of the diversity of communities and United Ways which in one way or another are trying to foster and support housing activities in their communities. While it may have been tempting to select only large cities with sophisticated CDCs, strong public and private sector support, and adequate technical assistance and project financing, it would not have effectively tested the various roles United Ways can play in addressing local housing needs. In addition, it would have significantly limited the involvement of smaller communities with less develop-ment capacity, and thus limited the overall impact throughout the United Way system.

O United Ways Are Being Looked to for More Than Financial Support.

The emergence of United Way in this area is seen as broadening the potential base of private sector support, and hopefully filling the long term operating support-needs of CDCs. In addition, institutional partners are looking to United Way for an increased role in public policy and advocacy and in helping to link housing development and social service delivery on the neighborhood level.

IV. **PROPOSAL**

United Way of America is requesting $760,000 over two years to support ongoing monitoring, technical assistance, and evaluation of the current Housing Initiatives Program Grantees; and to undertake specific information sharing, training and technical assistance activities aimed at increasing a dramatically greater number of United Ways' capacity and expanding their involvement in addressing the affordable housing problems in their communities.

United Way of America recently conducted a housing survey which uncovered a growing interest in this issue among nearly 200 United Ways. The goal of the effort is to build on the lessons learned in the demonstration sites and the momentum generated through increasing interest in this issue throughout the United Way system, to energize the system, further expand institutional impact and involve United Ways in housing, specifically in support of community development corporations.

A. GOALS AND OBJECTIVES

Building on the initial Housing Initiatives Program, the proposed two-year effort will be aimed at accomplishing the following goals:

O Expanding and enhancing United Ways' involvement and capacity in address-ing the affordable housing problems in their communities;

o Recognizing and elevating the achievements and roles of community develop-ment corporations in revitalizing distressed communities, and establishing a set of precedents for the ultimate affiliation of CDCs with United Way;

o   Educating the United Way technical assistance and support system to adapt its existing capabilities and resources to the specific needs of housing and community development corporations; and

o   Through United Way's access to community leadership, catalyzing the formation of housing collaboratives and partnerships on the local level, and attracting new funders and resources to support those efforts.

Specific program objectives and activities include the following:

1.   Providing ongoing monitoring, technical assistance and program oversight to current grantees; share lessons, learnings, and providing on-site technical assistance.

2.   Providing direct technical assistance to United Ways to build and institutionalize local capacity to meet the housing needs in their communities.

3.   Creating an information network and data base of individual United Ways involvement in housing activities -- successful strategies, techniques and innovations.

4.   Publishing a periodic newsletter, Housing Collaborative Guidebook, and other resource materials for distribution within the United Way system and for a broader audience of those in the field.

5.   Providing technical training and providing specific opportunities and forums for United Ways to share information on housing initiatives.

6.   Increasing United Ways involvement in public policy related to housing and community development, both nationally and locally.

7.   Generating greater awareness and understanding of the significant role CDCs can play in revitalizing distressed communities and increasing the number of CDCs that receive United Way support over both the shorter and longer terms.

8.   Working with national organizations to assess the social service delivery capacity of CDCs in some selected cities and developing and promoting models of integration of housing development and comprehensive neighborhood based services.

9. Conducting an evaluation of current Housing Initiatives Program activities and institutional impact, and preparing a Final Report.

B. WORKPLAN

The proposed workplan consists of several major components:

o   Ongoing Monitoring, Technical Assistance and Evaluation

Current Housing Initiatives Program Grants to the five demonstration sites extend through December 1991 so there is a need for ongoing monitoring and technical assistance by United Way of America through early 1992.

Ongoing support for United Way of America staff will:

-   Help facilitate program implementation and information sharing among Grantees and throughout the United Way system;

-   Increase the capacity to provide technical assistance to United Ways beyond the five demonstration cities; and

-   Continue to elevate, recognize and support the role of CDCs in housing and community development.

o   Specific activities include:

-   Conducting two grantee meetings per year;

-   Making two site visits per year to each demonstration site;

-   Facilitating information sharing through regular mailings; and putting together a Housing Collaborative guidebook outlining process, lessons learned, needed resources and various materials and workplans developed in demonstration cities.

-   United Way of America will also retain a consultant to design and conduct an initial evaluation of the demonstration program.

o   Increasing Institutionalization

United Way of America will:

110

- Continue to expand and institutionalize working relationships with other national organizations involved in housing and community development;

- Further expand its role in education and public policy; and

- Continue to recognize and elevate the role of the community development field and CDC leaders.

Some significant progress has been made in this area during the initial two years. When the Ford Foundation grant was awarded to United Way of America in 1987, there was relatively little involvement of United Ways in the area of affordable housing.

The number of local United Ways involved in any significant way in a housing program in their communities numbered less than ten. United Way of America had no staff expertise in this area, nor any public policy involvement or agenda. There has been significant change since that time.

The National Housing Advisory Committee, which was formulated to oversee the demonstration project, recently approved a Housing Policy Statement which was sent forward to United Way of America's Public Affairs Committee, a standing Board of Governor's Committee. The Public Affairs Committee approved the statement and set-up a Task Force on Affordable Housing to review legislative, regulatory and housing policy issues and make recommendations to United Way of America's Board of Governors. The adoption of the Housing Policy Statement will provide the framework for United Way of America to review and actively support passage of housing legislation. Paul Grogan, President of LISC, has agreed to serve on that Task Force.

United Way of America actively supported the extension of the Low-Income Housing Tax Credit. Edward Brennan, Chairman and Chief Executive Officer of Sears, Roebuck and Company, and Chairman of United Way of America's Board of Governors wrote individual letters to congressional sponsors in support of the extension. In addition, Richard O'Brien, United Way of America Executive Vice President and Chief Operating Officer, participated in a press conference on Capitol Hill in November 1989 in support of the permanent extension. Organizations like LISC and Enterprise can now call on United Way of America to join them in supporting this type of legislation, which had not and would not occur prior to this demonstration.

In addition, Ellen Gilligan recently served on a Task Force on Community/ Family Services for the Enterprise Foundation. The Task Force issued a report to the Foundation's Board which made specific recommendations regarding the integration of social service delivery with housing development. That report provided the impetus and framework for the Enterprise Foundation to establish a new Community Services Division. United Way of America has also used that report to further refine its thinking and promotion of the concept of comprehensive, wrap-around services. In this vein, during the next two years, United Way of America will work with LISC and the Enterprise Foundation to assess the social service delivery capacity of CDCs in two to four selected cities, and work to develop a plan to integrate social service delivery with new or existing housing development. This will further link United Ways with CDCs on the local level.

United Way of America recently conducted a Housing survey. The survey was sent to 482 communities where United Way raised more than $750,000. Responses from 218 local United Ways showed that nearly eighteen percent of United Ways responding rated their involvement and commitment to the issue of housing as top priority. Over sixty-two percent of the responses, or 135 United Ways, indicated some or considerable involvement and commitment to the issue, while less than ten percent had no involvement. Growing pressure of local housing needs contributes significantly to this response. However, United Way of America's Housing Initiatives Program and continued recognition of housing and community development as a legitimate area for United Way involvement also enhances this response.

Other institutional impact can be seen in the fact that United Way of America has developed an organizational Agenda and operational strategy around specific national initiatives. The operational strategy will focus on bringing cross-divisional support and cooperation to provide national leadership in developing policy and building collaborative relationships to address issues of national importance. United Way of America, in undertaking this effort, recognizes that social issues previously viewed as isolated problems are interconnected, and to help individuals and families become self-sufficient, we must take action in a number of areas. The lack of affordable housing is one of six key areas which United Way of America has identified as a national initiative. This indicates tremendous institutional change in little more than two years.

United Way of America is continuing to recognize and elevate the role of community development corporations and the importance of United Ways' involvement in the issue of low income housing. Some examples include:

- Having Jack Kemp speak to United Way of America's Board of Governors. Kemp is the first cabinet Secretary to address this group, and for some Board of Governors' members, it was a unique opportunity to see HUD in a new light and to view United Way's involvement in the issue of housing as an integral part of meeting human service needs.

- The role of CDCs has also been incorporated into two national conferences as major agenda items. The annual Volunteer Leaders Conference in Miami will feature a special breakfast program and tour of three Miami

CDCs. Speakers for the breakfast include: Bob Curvin; Paul Grogan, President of LISC; Otis Pitts, President of Tacolcy Economic Development Corporation; Graham Denton, Executive Vice President of NCNB of Florida; and Jim Rouse, Chairman of the Enterprise Foundation. The program is by invitation only to United Way of America Board of Governors, and Chief Volunteers and Executives in United Way's 30 major markets. This is the first time this subject has been presented to this level of leadership within the United Way system.

- Following up on that, Bill Aramony, President of United Way of America, will present personal recognition awards to three outstanding CDC directors at our biennial Staff Leaders Conference in May 1990. The awards will be small cash awards, focusing on the achievements of CDCs which combine housing development with social service delivery. We envision using LISC, the Enterprise Foundation and the National Congress for Community Development to nominate potential recipients. While United Way has given awards to individuals, in the past, they have not been cash awards, and have never focused on individuals working in housing and community development.

    The awards will be presented at a general session of the conference and will receive high visibility.

    United Way of America will continue to elevate and highlight the issue of housing and the role of CDCs in its publications, and at regional and national conferences and in "how to" and "best practices" guidebooks.

Increase United Way Capacity/Further Enhance Institutional Relationships

The bulk of activity during the next two years will be under the general heading of building United Way capacity and further enhancing institutional relationships in the area of housing and community development.

United Way of America plans to focus its activities on those United Ways responding to its survey which indicated some or considerable involvement in the area of housing and those that rated it a top priority. The survey highlighted a specific need for technical training and information sharing among United Ways. United Way of America will address these needs by undertaking the following specific activities:

- Conducting six to eight cluster meetings of United Ways --convening similar size United Ways to share information about housing programs and policy; specific information presented by the Housing Initiatives Program

113

Grantees about how to establish a local housing collaborative, how to get volunteer board support and approval, identifying and securing new resources to support the effort; and lessons learned. We anticipate involving 100 or more United Ways in these meetings.

- Using the initial information gathered in the Housing Survey, United Way of America will retain the Community Information Exchange to develop a data base profiling 35 to 50 local United Ways' involvement in housing. That information can be put on our Human Care Network, an existing computerized network linking United Ways and distributed in written form throughout the system.

- United Way of America will develop, publish and distribute a series of resource materials to increase technical knowledge, promote information-sharing and highlight United Way involvement. Such materials include a periodic newsletter, published three to four times per year, a Housing Collaborative Guidebook, Supplemental Housing Strategies, as follow-up to our highly successful *Raising the Roof*, published in conjunction with the Community Information Exchange. United Way of America will also produce a ten-minute video on Housing Initiatives for use throughout the system.

- Providing on-site technical assistance to local United Ways. Project staff as well as consultants will be used to provide specific on-site technical assistance.

- Designing and conducting a week-long course on Housing Initiatives through our National Academy for Voluntarism (NAV). NAV is United Way of America's national training arm which each year attracts about 2,200 local United Way professionals to a variety of one-week courses. In this case, we would envision using technical experts such as the Development Training Institute, LISC, the Enterprise Foundation, as well as those United Ways currently involved in Housing Initiatives as part of the faculty. This course is envisioned as a basic introductory course focusing on: housing policy; the low-income housing delivery system; financing sources and resources needed to support low income housing; the emergence of community development corporations; and, planning and implementing a program -- roles for United Way.

- Conducting a series of one-day local seminars with United Ways and local housing providers and CDCs. In cooperation with the National Congress for Community Economic Development, United Way of America will help local United Ways design and conduct one-day workshops focused on a particular technical topic. Such topics might include: Community Reinvestment; Housing Trust Funds; or the Low-Income Housing Tax Credit. These workshops would provide the opportunity for local United Ways to convene a broadbased group, and facilitate increased technical knowledge. They will also provide the opportunity to begin to link United Ways and their corporate volunteers with housing providers on the local level.

- Identify two to four selected communities to assess social service delivery capacity of CDCs, social service gaps and needs in CDC-served areas, and create a model or process to further link CDCs with United Way and United Way-funded agencies in the delivery of comprehensive social services in their neighborhoods.

Working with the Housing Advisory Committee and the Public Affairs Committee, devise a strategy and workplan for increasing local United Ways and United Way state organizations' role in public policy and advocacy. Such plans might include identifying opportunities for testimony on specific legislation in Congress and state legislatures; convening specific housing policy meetings for state and local United Ways and integrating housing policy into regularly scheduled public affairs and government relations regional workshops.

- Continue to promote and recognize a greater awareness and understanding of the role of CDCs and the link between United Way's goals and mission and those of CDCs. This would be done by utilizing opportunities to feature CDCs and housing activities in annual conferences, regional workshops and forums; United Way of America publications and promotional materials.

- Conduct an evaluation of current Housing Initiatives Program activities and institutional impact, and prepare a Final Report. United Way of America, with direction from the National Advisory Committee, will retain a consultant to design and conduct an evaluation of the initial Housing Initiatives Program and prepare a Final Report which can be distributed throughout the system and to a broader audience of those in the field.

V. STAFFING, OVERSIGHT AND GOVERNANCE

The project will be administered by the Community Initiatives Division.

Community Initiatives is part of the United Way Support Group which also includes the Resource Development, Field Services and National Corporate Leadership Divisions.

Community Initiatives, with a staff of 30 people, is responsible for developing programs and providing leadership and support to local United Ways in areas of Community Problem Solving and Needs Assessment, Information and Referral, Literacy, Inclusiveness, Fund Distribution, AIDS, Childcare, Housing, Aging and Volunteer and Outreach Services. Community Initiatives also administers the federally-funded Emergency Food and Shelter Program.

The division also currently administers grants from the Gannett, Kellogg, Exxon, American Express, Coca-Cola, and Levi Strauss Foundations, and the Federal Government.

The project will be overseen at the management level by the divisional Vice President, Thomas M. Nunan. Ellen Gilllgan, Project Director, will have day-to-day program management responsibilities. She will be assisted by a technical assistance coordinator and a secretary.

United Way of America is led by a 35-member, volunteer Board of Governors. Its 350-member staff is led by President William Aramony; chief Operating Officer is Richard J.O'Brien. The organization, composed of five major groups, plus a senior vice president responsible for liaison with all major national health and human service organizations and with organized labor. It has affiliates in 20 foreign countries and will be co-sponsoring conferences in Moscow and Poland this year.

Chief Financial Officer for the organization is Thomas Merlo. Ray Boyer, Senior Staff Accountant, who reports to Mr. Merlo has responsibility for accounting and financial reporting for the project.

The Housing Initiatives Program is overseen by a 21-member volunteer National Advisory Committee chaired by Larry D. Horner, Chairman and CEO of Peat, Marwick, Main and member of United Way of America's Board of Governors. Mr. Horner is responsible for oversight of the program from the Board level, and reports on program progress and policy recommendations at semi-annual Board meetings. As noted earlier, the Public Affairs Committee will also be developing a role for itself and United Way of America as it relates to housing through a specially appointed Task Force, which will report and make recommendations to the Board of Governors. The Public Affairs Committee is chaired by John J. Phelan, Jr., Chairman and Chief Executive Officer, New York Stock Exchange The emergence of the Public Affairs Task Force on Housing will raise the awareness, visibility and involvement of United Way of America's Board of Governors in this issue and program.

PROPOSED BUDGET

April 1, 1990 - March 31, 1992

Personnel:	YEAR 1	YEAR 2	TOTAL
Project Director (90%)	$50,400	$53,360	$103,760
Technical Assistance			
Coordinator	28,000	31,000	59,000
Secretary (100%)	20,000	21,000	41,000
Fringe Benefits (30%)	29,520	31,608	61,128
Sub-Total	$127,920	$136,968	$264,888
Evaluation:	$20,000	$20,000	$40,000
Conferencing:			
Cluster Meetings	30,000	30,000	60,000
(6-8) 2-Day Meetings			
40 People Per Meeting			
1 Day Technical	7,500	7,500	15,000
Seminars (5)			
Grantee Meetings	7,000	7,000	14,000
2 Per Year			
NAV Course	5,000	5,000	10,000
Sub-Total	$69,500	$69,500	$139,000
Resource Materials:			
Database (50 Profiles)	$20,000	$ -0-	$ 20,000
Newsletter	5,000	7,000	12,000
Guidebook (1000 Copies)	-0-	25,000	25,000
Video	-0-	35,000	35,000
Final Report	-0-	10,000	10,000
Sub-Total	$25,000	$77,000	$102,000
Social Service Delivery			
Assessment (4 Cities):	$30,000	$30,000	$60,000

WINNING GRANT PROPOSALS

Consultants (125 Days at $400 Per Day):	50,000	50,000	100,000
Travel:	25,000	25,000	50,000
	$105,000	$105,000	$210,000
Sub-Total	$327,420	$388,468	$715,888
Overhead	$22,056	$22,056	$44,112
Total Request	$349,476	$410,524	$760,000
UWA In-Kind Overhead	(49,532)	(49,532)	

NOTE: United Way of America's overhead rate is 20% of direct costs which includes: Finance and Administration, Space, Equipment, Telephone, Postage and Supplies.

Success with a Local Business I:
University of Washington Attracts Campaign Grant Through Scholarships

The Institution: The University of Washington (UW) is one of America's leading universities. Approximately 33,500 students enrolled in the University's sixteen schools and colleges are taught by a faculty that includes four Nobel laureates and numerous other world class scholars. Since 1975, UW has ranked first among all universities in federal funds for research and training. For over two decades, UW has had programs to promote diversity among its student body and faculty. (Minority student representation is approximately twenty-three percent.) The Office of Minority Affairs (OMA) administers programs to recruit ethnic minority and economically disadvantaged students and provide them support services to help them succeed. It also conducts outreach programs to encourage early college preparation for middle-school students from underrepresented minority groups.

The Author: Barbara Noseworthy wrote this proposal while employed as the Assistant Director of Corporation and Foundation Relations at the University of Washington. Currently, she serves as Director of Development Programs at Whitman College, a private liberal arts college in Walla Walla, Washington.

Background: After exploring UW and First Interstate relationships and mutual interests, they determined that a program in the UMA most closely matched their interests. UW tested the First Interstate Vice President's response to a seven-figure request. Although significantly higher than what she was considering, she agreed to review a draft $1 million proposal. In this way, they determined that the project matched the company's interests and goals. When it was evident that First Interstate would be unable to contribute $1 million to support three centers, but clearly supported the project, UW submitted a second draft proposal for $750,000 to support two centers. "Throughout the process, we worked with the First Interstate Vice President to prepare a reasonable payout schedule, decide how best to involve our volunteers, and verify that we were proceeding in an acceptable manner," writes Ms. Noseworthy. "When the final proposal was submitted, it was almost certain to be approved." Credited for her essential role was Lynn Hogan, former Director of Corporation and Foundation Relations, who was responsible for all stages of prospect development. "A proposal does not make its case in isolation. The strength of the institution and leadership from the Regents, President, and Vice President for Minority Affairs are equally, if not more important."

PROPOSAL TO FIRST INTERSTATE BANK OF WASHINGTON

FROM THE UNIVERSITY OF WASHINGTON

NOVEMBER 1990

TABLE OF CONTENTS

EXECUTIVE SUMMARY

The University of Washington and First Interstate Bank of Washington have had a historic partnership. For more than a decade, First Interstate regularly has contributed to several of the University's programs including the School of Business Administration; the public radio station, KUOW; and the Educational Opportunity Program for minority and economically disadvantaged students. For the past five years, First Interstate Bank of Washington has provided scholarships to outstanding freshmen students attending the University who graduated from a Washington high school.

In addition to its financial support, First Interstate executives and directors provide their expertise and leadership to the University of Washington. For example, _____. chairman and chief executive officer, serves on the advisory board of the Graduate School of Business Administration. _____ and _____, directors of First Interstate, are Regents of the University of Washington. Another director, _____, serves as a volunteer with the University's first major fund drive, the Campaign for Washington.

Strategically located on the Pacific Rim, First Interstate Bank of Washington and the University of Washington are in a region of rapid growth and expansion. The population of the area is projected to increase from 2.2 million to 3.3 million by the year 2010. This tremendous growth over the next twenty years will create new opportunities and challenges. Economic opportunity both for our state and our region will remain closely tied to the strength of our educational resources. First Interstate Bank of Washington and the University of Washington share a commitment to invest in and develop one of this region's greatest resources: its people.

As a public institution, the University of Washington is committed to providing the state of Washington with well-educated citizens. The University has established programs aimed at both increasing access to education by students who come from minority or economically disadvantaged backgrounds and improving the quality of education in our nation's schools. The Early Scholars Outreach Program, for example, provides academic support to minority students who have been identified, at an early age, as having the potential to succeed in college. As part of the University's Office of Minority Affairs, the Program is offered in seven middle schools across the state including schools in eastern Washington and the Olympic peninsula.

The University of Washington is in the midst of its first major fund drive, the Campaign for Washington, with a goal of raising $250 million in private gifts and pledges by 1992. The Campaign is necessary to maintain the quality of graduates and research that this state and this region have come to expect of the University of Washington.

This proposal recognizes our shared commitment to developing our region's human capital. We are pleased to present this campaign proposal to First Interstate Bank of Washington and ask that you consider directing a gift of $_____ as follows:

A. <u>First Interstate Young Scholars Program</u> $_____

To establish programs, modelled after and administered through the Early Scholars Outreach Program, for students in two public middle schools.

AND

B. <u>First Interstate Endowed Scholarships</u> $_____

To establish scholarships for minority or economically disadvantaged students, with initial priority given to students who participated in the First Interstate Young Scholars Program.

AN OUTSTANDING UNIVERSITY

The University of Washington is one of the leading universities in the United States, with a teaching and research faculty known nationally and internationally for its accomplishments. In 1989, Hans Dehmelt, professor of physics, received the Nobel Prize in Physics. Two 1990 Nobel laureates, E. Donnall Thomas in Medicine, and William G. Sharpe in Economic Science, have affiliations with the University. Since 1984, thirty-three junior faculty members have been chosen by the National Science Foundation as Presidential Young Investigators, an award designed to honor the nation's most promising scientists and engineers. Thirty-two senior faculty members have received Guggenheim Fellowships since 1980. As of 1989, thirty faculty members have been elected to the National Academy of Sciences, five faculty members have been elected to the National Academy of Engineering, and seventeen of the University's faculty are members of the American Academy of Arts and Sciences.

Another measure of the strength of the University is its research record. For over two decades, the University consistently has ranked among the nation's top five institutions, public and private, in receipt of federal research awards. It has ranked first among public institutions in this same category every year since 1977, and currently receives more than $345 million annually to support its research and training programs.

While research discoveries make headlines, the University's most important contributions to the state and region are the educated men and women who graduate each year: approximately 5,000 students with baccalaureate degrees, more than 1,700 with master's degrees, over 300 Ph.D.'s. and almost 400 physicians, lawyers, dentists, and pharmacists.

THE CAMPAIGN FOR WASHINGTON

The University of Washington is in the midst of its first major fund drive, the Campaign for Washington, with a goal of raising $250 million in private gifts and pledges by 1992. Half of this goal will provide support for faculty and students through endowed chairs, professorships, graduate fellowships, and undergraduate scholarships. The other half will provide new or enhanced facilities or equipment and will support current activities in the University's schools and colleges.

The Campaign for Washington is a campus-wide effort, whose goal was arrived at through a consultative process involving Regents, administrators, deans, faculty members, volunteers, and donors to the University.

In preparing for this fund drive, many important issues were raised, including the question of whether a public university should seek private funds at this level. The consensus was not only that we should but that we must. Any university, public or private, which does not have the endowment and facilities to support its best faculty and students will not continue to rank among the best in the country.

Private support for the University of Washington is an investment by corporations, foundations, and individuals who recognize the University of Washington as a valuable resource, not only for the state but also for the nation. Through the Campaign for Washington, the University is asking friends, alumni, corporations, and foundations to invest in a future for the University as distinguished as its past.

FIRST INTERSTATE YOUNG SCHOLARS PROGRAM

Background

A major challenge facing all of education -- from elementary schools to university classrooms -- is to encourage minority students to graduate from high school, pursue undergraduate and advanced degrees, and become role models for the next generation.

The University of Washington is vitally involved in the issues of basic education in a multicultural society. In 1987, the University formed a partnership with seven public middle schools with large minority enrollments to address the severe under-representation of minority students graduating from the state's higher education institutions. As part of the University's Office of Minority Affairs, the Early Scholars Outreach Program (ESOP) provides academic support to minority middle school students (6th-8th grade) who have the potential to succeed in college.

The immediate goal of Early Scholars Outreach Program is to increase the number of minority students who, by ninth grade, are enrolled in college preparatory coursework. Long-term goals include increasing the number of minority students who graduate from high school fully prepared to enter a college or university and, ultimately, increasing the number of minority students who graduate from a college or university. By encouraging these students -- at an early age -- to take college preparatory coursework and demonstrating that pursuing a college education is viable for them, we hope to address the problem of high minority student attrition in higher education.

As part of the Early Scholars Outreach Program, the participating students are matched with a college student, usually from a similar background, who serves as a role model, tutor, and mentor to several ESOP students. The ESOP students meet twice a week with their tutor-mentor to work on homework problems; improve their reading, writing, and math skills; foster a greater sense of self-esteem; and prepare themselves for the pressures and rigorous coursework they can expect at a major research institution. Other components of the ESOP include: campus visits and tours of local businesses for ESOP students; support programs for parents; and an intensive summer program for 8th grade students to strengthen their skills in mathematics, reading, writing, computers, and study skills prior to entering the 9th grade.

During 1989-90 more than 135 students participated in the Early Scholars Outreach Program, which currently serves Meany, Eckstein, and Whitman middle schools in Seattle; McKnight and Nelsen middle schools in Renton; Harrison Middle School in Yakima; and the Taholah School (Quinault Reservation) on the Olympic peninsula. The core funding for this program is provided by the Washington State legislature. Many parents, teachers, and administrators, however, have requested that the Early Scholars Outreach Program be offered in their schools. In Seattle alone, seven middle schools are unable to participate and 73 students currently are on a waiting list due to funding limitations.

Proposal

We are requesting a gift to establish the First Interstate Young Scholars

Program for minority or economically disadvantaged students in two public middle schools. The greater part of the First Interstate Young Scholars Program would be modelled after and administered through the Early Scholars Outreach Program and would include weekly tutoring and academic sessions between the students and their tutor-mentors, tours of local businesses, and campus visits. Programs for parents might explore strategies for motivating and encouraging their children to do better in school, working with their child at home to improve his or her study skills, and stress management.

The First Interstate Young Scholars Program

The First Interstate Young Scholars Program would be offered in two Washington middle schools with large minority student enrollments. The following schools would be considered: in Yakima, Washington Middle School; and in Seattle, South Shore, Denny, or Washington middle schools. Each school has expressed a strong interest in participating in such a program. At each school, 50-60 students annually would participate.

The director of the Early Scholars Outreach Program also would serve as the program director of the First Interstate Young Scholars Program. At each of the selected schools, an area coordinator (usually a teacher or counselor) would manage the day-to-day activities and the supervision of tutors. Each tutor would work with five or six students. Students would be selected based on the recommendation of their teachers or counselors. In addition to minority students, children from economically disadvantaged backgrounds would be encouraged to participate in the First Interstate Young Scholars Program.

Students who have completed the 8th grade would participate in an intensive academic enrichment program during the summer. Students from the Seattle middle school would come to the University of Washington campus for four weeks to improve their mathematics, computer, language, and study skills. Students attend classes five days a week four hours each day. The summer program for First Interstate Young Scholars in Yakima would be tailored to the specific needs of the students from this area. For example, depending on the season, many of these students spend part of each day working in the fields and orchards and would not be able to attend a four-week program in Seattle.

The Program Director would work with the Area Coordinator in Yakima to design the summer program, which would occur at a central site in Yakima and probably would involve two weeks of intensive coursework.

First Interstate Involvement

The Program Director would establish an advisory board, composed of First Interstate representatives, parents, school representatives, and other members of the community. This volunteer board would meet quarterly to review the program's activities, make recommendations, and offer support and guidance to the program.

At each of the selected schools, the Area Coordinator would closely work with a First Interstate employee who has been designated the contact person for the First Interstate Young Scholars Program in their community. Together they would seek opportunities for First Interstate employees to become involved with the program. For example, First Interstate employees might serve as mentors to individual students, plan activities for parents and students, chaperone weekend activities such as a trip to the Pacific Science Center, or assist with visits to the University of Washington.

Additional Support Programs for First Interstate Young Scholars

During their high school years, the First Interstate Young Scholars would be encouraged to participate in two programs designed to enable students from minority or economically disadvantaged backgrounds to graduate from high school and pursue a college education. Funded by the U.S. Department of Education, Upward Bound offers year-round tutoring, classroom instruction, an intensive summer program and other student activities at more than 400 locations throughout the country. In Seattle, Upward Bound is offered through the University of Washington's Office of Minority Affairs, the North Seattle Community College, and the City of Seattle (each program serves different high schools). Upward Bound also is administered through the Yakima Valley Community College.

The Educational Talent Search program provides information and one-on-one counseling to high school students about the logistics of attending a university or college. The staff work directly with students and their families to complete application forms, obtain financial assistance, prepare for the Scholastic Aptitude Tests, and other activities. The University's Office of Minority Affairs sponsors the Educational Talent Search program in Seattle. The program also is administered through the Yakima Valley Opportunities Industrialization Center.

In addition to Educational Talent Search and Upward Bound for high school students, the University's Office of Minority Affairs provides a variety of services for undergraduate students such as tutoring, academic and personal counseling, financial aid, an alumni mentoring program (in conjunction with the Alumni Association), and other activities. The Early Identification Program (EIP) is designed to encourage and prepare minority or economically disadvantaged students to attend graduate school, and includes early exposure to research processes, faculty mentors, seminars, advising, and assistance with graduate school applications.

Evaluation

Several measures would be used to evaluate the First Interstate Young Scholars Program including: students' grade point averages; student, parent, tutor, and teacher evaluations; attendance at tutorial sessions; attendance in school; tracking the number of students who, by the ninth grade, have enrolled in college preparatory coursework; and monitoring the students through high school to determine how many continue college preparatory coursework and enroll in a college or university.

Acknowledgement

During November 1990, the staff in the Early Scholars Outreach Program presented their findings at the National Higher Education Conference on Black Student Retention held in Washington D.C. They will seek additional opportunities to present and publish the activities and results of the First Interstate Young Scholars Program in professional journals and at state and national meetings. All publications and brochures relating to this program shall recognize the support of the First Interstate Bank of Washington.

As part of the Early Scholars Outreach Program, participating students receive a shirt with the ESOP logo on it. Students wear their ''scholar shirt'' on days when there will be a field trip and at other times. By identifying with a unique group of scholars, the participants are made to feel special; their self-esteem and motivation are enhanced. Students in the First Interstate Young Scholars Program would receive a ''scholar shirt'' especially designed for the program.

Continuation

The Office of Minority Affairs would seek support from both public and private sources to continue this demonstration program after the initial five-year period. With several of the schools that participate in the Early Scholars Outreach Program (ESOP), the local school district has provided enhancement support to the ESOP. The private-public partnership demonstrated by the First Imerstate Young Scholars Proaram would assist the Office of Minority Affairs in seeking long-term support from the state legislature, the Superintendent of Public Instruction, or other public sources.

During the first three years of the First Interstate Young Scholars Program, the staff also would establish relationships with corporations and foundations that would be likely to support the program after its initial demonstration phase is complete.

FIRST INTERSTATE ENDOWED SCHOLARSHIPS
For Minority or Economically Disadvantaged Students from Washington State

Background

Maintaining a diverse student body and enabling students from every part of our society to achieve their potential are important goals of the University of Washington. These goals are supported through active efforts to recruit students who are members of racial and ethnic minority groups to attend the University. Unfortunately, the University currently is limited in its ability to offer scholarships that would encourage talented minority and economically disadvantaged students to attend.

The Office of Minority Affairs provides a variety of services to bring minority and economically disadvantaged students to the University of Washington, and to support them while they attend. These services include recruitment, admissions, advising, tutoring, personal and career counseling, and financial assistance. In addition to assisting students during their undergraduate years, a special program -- the Early Scholars Outreach Program -- is designed to encourage and prepare 6th, 7th, and 8th grade students from minority backgrounds to pursue a college preparatory curriculum in high school. The Program includes weekly tutorials in several subjects as well as academic and personal counseling from their tutor-mentors, most of whom are University of Washington students from similar backgrounds.

Higher education has opened avenues of opportunity to millions of Americans, yet many minority and economically disadvantaged students have not pursued higher education because of financial need, lack of preparation, and other factors.

While students with demonstrated financial need ordinarily receive federal and state financial aid, there often is a difference between the amount of aid awarded and the real costs of attending the University. This gap may prevent many minority and economically disadvantaged students from even considering attending the University of Washington.

Scholarships that emphasize academic performance while in high school would provide an important incentive to minority and economically disadvantaged students to enroll in college preparatory coursework and do well in school. The availability of scholarships also would demonstrate to these students that pursuing a college education is a realistic option for them.

Proposal

We propose a gift to establish the First Interstate Endowed Scholarships for Minority or Economically Disadvantaged Students from Washington State. The First Interstate Scholarships would increase the University's ability to recruit and support the state's most talented minority and economically disadvantaged students who otherwise might not be able to attend the University of Washington.

These Scholarships, which could be awarded on the basis of academic merit alone, or a combination of academic merit and financial need, could be awarded to students in any field of study, for one year or for a longer period. The income from this endowment would be used to cover the costs of tuition, fees, books and supplies, and other educational expenses. Initial priority would be given to Washington high school students who have participated in the First Interstate Young Scholars Program.

Success with a Local Business II:
Stonehill College Banks on Scholarships

The Institution: The Holy Cross Fathers established Stonehill College in 1948, continuing the tradition they started over a hundred years ago with the founding of the University of Notre Dame in South Bend, Indiana. A fully accredited coeducational, comprehensive college, Stonehill is committed to offering its 1,850 students a full range of educational and extracurricular activities at an affordable price. Small classes, a dedicated faculty, a beautiful campus, traditional Catholic values, a sense of community and a great location are the other reasons Stonehill says it attracts approximately 480 freshmen students from over 3,800 applicants every year. Currently, 84% of Stonehill's freshmen students who filed for aid received financial assistance in the form of scholarships, loans or work-study.

The Author: George Hagerty is currently the Director of Corporate, Foundation and Government Relations and Associate Professor of Political Science and Education at Stonehill College. The author of twenty-five book chapters, articles and public reports on public policy, teacher education, school finance and the education of children and youth with disabilities, Dr. Hagerty recieved his B.A. in international affairs from Stonehill, and his masters and doctoral degrees from Harvard University in educational administration. He has served in a number of administrative posts in the U.S. Department of Education and is a member of the Massachusetts Council on Disabilities by gubernatorial appointment. In addition to his work at Stonehill, he is a lecturer at Harvard and a frequent speaker and consultant to national organizations and state governments in the areas of education policy and school finance.

Background: An initial contact was made through a chance social meeting between one of the Holy Cross Fathers and an executive of the State Street Bank and Trust Company, who expressed the company's interest in promoting the diversification of the banking industry, especially by assisting inner-city groups. This was followed by a series of meetings with officers of the bank between Dr. Haggerty, the chairman of the business department, and the bank's office of community affairs. After discussing the company's needs and Stonehill College's capabilities, the College sent a draft proposal to the bank. This was refined following subsequent discussions and was followed by a final proposal. This was the first gift from the bank to Stonehill College and the entire process, from initial contact to funding, took only six months.

February 26, 1993

Mr. George A. Bowman
Vice President
Community Affairs
State Street Bank and Trust Company
225 Franklin Street
Boston, Massachusetts 02110-2804

Dear Mr. Bowman,

On behalf of Stonehill College, it is my privilege to submit a proposal for the inauguration of the *State Street Scholars in Business Program*. As you will come to learn through your review of the enclosed materials, this proposal and the programming which it envisions are the product of initiative and the spirit of cooperation. George Hagerty, Bill Burke and Father Tom Gariepy have told me of the valuable counsel and support which you and Mr. Russell have provided in the preparation of this submission. For this, and for the consideration which you and other State Street officials are extending with respect to this initiative, I am sincerely grateful.

It is important for you to know that the *State Street Scholars Program* is pivotal to the College's plan to establish a pluralistic community -- a community dedicated to both excellence and equity. With your guidance we believe that we have fashioned a comprehensive program which provides both the support and the academic and experiential preparation for minority students who seek careers in business and finance. We are particularly excited about the prospect of recruiting and educating students who wish to pursue accounting careers. As our proposal conveys, Stonehill is able to provide these students with the specialized accounting and technology-based preparation central to a successful career in today's challenging international marketplace.

Briefly, our proposal offers the following opportunities:

> **Business Challenge:** Under the terms of individualized coopera-
> tive agreements, Stonehill business faculty will assist in educational
> and recruitment activities at six ''paired'' high schools selected from
> the City of Boston, Suffolk County, and Quincy. Stonehill faculty will
> develop specialized on-site programming for teachers and students
> -- programming which is designed to spark curricular innovation and
> career interest, especially among students from minority back-
> grounds;

135

Explore!: Those students selected to participate in the *State Street Business Program* will be invited to participate in a one-month academic and social orientation program prior to their entry to Stonehill College. This program, which will be a contributed service by the College, will aid *State Street Scholars* in their transition from secondary school to undergraduate study. Each *State Street Scholar* will be enrolled in two three-credit courses - one an introductory business course, and the second a class adopted from Stonehill's successful undergraduate learning theory and evaluation course, Learning to Learn; and

State Street Scholars: Stonehill proposes to recruit and retain a minimum of twelve minority students designated as *State Street Scholars*. These students will be recruited from ''paired schools'' in the *Business Challenge Program*, as well as other high schools and community college programs located in eastern Massachusetts, New Hampshire and Maine. The College commits the financial assistance necessary to ensure that *State Street Scholars* can successfully matriculate and complete Stonehill's undergraduate program.

For this program, we are requesting an award of $48,000 from the State Street Foundation for a period of four years. Thus, the total requested for the period July 1, 1993 through June 30, 1997 is $192,000. We expect that continued funding (that is, annual awards on and after July 1, 1994) will be made based upon the submission of a continuation request and proof of the College's progress in attaining the program's objectives.

If we may provide further information to assist in your evaluation of this proposal, please do not hesitate to contact me or George Hagerty ((508) 230-1029).

With best wishes and appreciation for your consideration, I remain

Sincerely,

Bartley MacPhaidin, C.S.C.
President

A Prospectus

The State Street Scholars in Business Program:
A program of Educational Outreach to Attract and to Prepare Future Generations of Inner City Students for Careers in Accounting and Related Business Disciplines

Stonehill College
North Easton, Massachusetts

An Overview: Stonehill College offers a learning environment that joins the rich inheritance of a liberal education with the professional and technical knowledge necessary for leadership in a rapidly changing and competitive world. *The State Street Scholars in Business Program* is an effort on the part of the Stonehill community to encourage and support the pursuit of business careers (particularly in the field of accounting but also in the areas of finance management and marketing) among students who are residents of the cities of Quincy and Boston.

The *State Street Scholars in Business* program will be comprised of three interrelated offerings: (1) *Business Challenge* (a program of business career exploration and encouragement for high school students and their teachers); (2) *Explore!* (a pre-enrollment summer program for inner city students admitted to Stonehill College --designed to promote the acquisition of the entry-level academic skills essential to success in undergraduate study); and (3) *State Street Scholars* (the administration of an internship-enriched program in accounting and related business fields for students from inner city backgrounds).

The State Street Scholars in Business Program: The three major program elements proposed for the *State Street Scholars* are detailed below:

> *Business Challenge:* Successful business careers begin with knowledge -- knowledge of career options as well as the education and experiences necessary for entry into business professions. Through *Business Challenge*, Stonehill's business faculty will be paired with selected high schools located in the cities of Boston and Quincy.

> Under the terms of this cooperative arrangement faculty members will: (1) participate in regularly-scheduled business lectures and other student-based classroom activities designed to introduce high school students to the many professional options available in ac-

counting and related business disciplines; (2) encourage students to explore business career options through the scheduling and supervision of individual and small group visits to local companies; (3) motivate students (and their parents) to investigate careers in accounting and related disciplines through the administration of a school-based business forum -- a lecture series to which business leaders will be invited to address career-molding issues; and (4) provide to high school teachers inservice training in business-related areas with a special emphasis on the business applications of new technologies. By October 1st of each year the Stonehill faculty member will in consultation with the school's administration develop an annual action plan which will detail the scope nature and timelines of the Business Challenge activities to be conducted during the academic year.

The selection of ''paired'' *Business Challenge* high schools will be determined by mutual agreement between *State Street Bank* and Stonehill College;

To aid in the equitable selection of *Business Challenge* high schools a letter of invitation/interest will be forwarded to all Boston and Quincy high schools indicating the *Business Challenge* opportunity and seeking an expression of interest;

A breakfast meeting with interested high school representatives will be convened in May 1993 at the *State Street Bank* headquarters at which time the *Business Challenge* program will be announced by Bank and Stonehill representatives. (Since *State Street Scholars* will also be recruited from the region's community colleges one representative of each of eastern Massachusetts' Community Colleges will be invited to attend this introductory meeting (these schools will include but not be limited to: Bunker Hill Community College, Roxbury Community College, Quincy College Massasoit Community College and Bristol Community College);

Final selection of ''paired'' *Business Challenge* schools will be determined after Stonehill (in consultation with *State Street Bank* officials) reviews proposals submitted by each high school interested in competing for *Business Challenge* participation. These proposals will be due to the College's Program Coordinator by July 1 1993;

An important component of the *Business Challenge* program will be on-site visitation by students high school, faculty, community college and Stonehill faculty to State Street facilities to observe first-hand the vast array of business applications for new technologies. In addition the College will attempt to video-record these on-site experiences and to edit this material into training videos which can be distributed to schools and colleges beyond those which will participate in the *State Street Scholars Program in Business*;

Explore!: The transition from secondary school to college can prove a harrowing experience for any student. This is particularly true for the inner city students Stonchill seeks to recruit as State Street Scholars. With the institution's experience as a guide the Stonehill community has come to learn that the undergraduate success of inner city students is a function not only of the academic and social support that they receive on campus **during** their college years but (as study after study has attested) it is a function of their **preparation** for the college environment and its demands, as well.

With the assistance of ''matching'' grant resources Stonehill will implement a summer program *Explore!* for students selected as *State Street Scholars* to ease their transition to undergraduate study. The program to be scheduled each August will provide *State Street Scholars* with a solid academic and social orientation as well as a comprehensive introduction to the College's resources and ''student-centered'' academic and personal support systems. Each *State Street Scholar* will be enrolled in two three-credit courses, one an introductory business course and the second a class adapted from Stonehill's successful undergraduate learning theory and evaluation course, <u>Learning to Learn</u>;

State Street Scholars: Each year Stonehill College will endeavor to recruit and admit from Boston, Quincy and other urban neighborhoods a minimum of twelve (12) and a maximum of fifteen (15) minority undergraduate students each of whom will be recognized as *State Street Scholars*. To be designated as a *State Street Scholar* eligible students must possess an interest in pursuing a career in business (including accounting, finance, management, and marketing). Scholars may be selected for participation in the program at any time during their undergraduate experience (i.e. during their freshman, sophomore, junior, or senior year); additionally participants may be selected for involvement in the program from a period of one to four years as individual circumstances warrant. To remain in the program students must be in good academic standing (attaining a cumulative average of 2.0 or above).

State Street Scholars will participate in a comprehensive educational program to prepare them for: (1) leadership in the business community especially in financial accounting and computer accounting and/or (2) further graduate or professional sludy in their chosen field (e.g., accounting, business administration). The components of the program will be integrated into the Scholars' undergraduate course of study and will include:

> The development of an individualized business education plan for each Scholar which identifies career interests and objectives as well as the most effective means for addressing these interests and objectives (e.g., coursework, internship experiences, summer employment);

> Participation in a regularly-scheduled seminar through which invited guests will address issues essential to leadership in business. The majority of these seminars will be lead by business people, practitioners and experts who are responsible on a daily basis for critical management decisions and the long-term well-being of a corporation or small business;

> Under the guidance of a program coordinator and based on the Scholar's business education plan students will receive ongoing individualized academic and career-oriented counseling. Special attention will be devoted to the selection of coursework and internship options which will allow the Scholar to explore professional interests and to achieve career options;

> During each *Scholar's* junior year the student will participate in a one semester Bank-sponsored internship at the State Street Bank headquarters;

> During each *Scholar's* senior year the student will participate in a Bank-sponsored international internship at a *State Street Bank* overseas facility or foreign *State Street Bank* affiliate;

> In the event that the five year program (required after 1998 for those wishing to sit for the CPA exam) is implemented at

Stonehill prior to 1997 additional *State Street Bank* sponsored internship activities will be available for each *Scholar* during the ''fifth year'' of study.

Specialized programming offered each semester by Stonehill's Office of Career Services to ensure that all career-related expectations can be reasonably achieved (e.g., programming will include targeted career exploration opportunities, resume development, interview preparation and scheduling and the pursuit of employment/graduate school ''matches'').

A Request for Support: Stonehill College requests that the officers of the State Street Bank and Trust Company consider a grant of $48 000 to support the activities associated with the *State Street Scholars in Business Program* for academic year (AY) 1993-94. It is the college's hope that this program will receive annual support for a period of four years (i.e., from AY 1993-94 through AY 1996-97) at which time Stonehill will accept full responsibility for the financing and operation of the Program. Thus the total program cost for the State Street Scholars in Business Program will be $192,000. Funding for AY 1994-95 through AY 1996-97 will be awarded upon the submission of an annual request and proof of the College's progress in meeting program objectives.

The costs to be assumed annually by State Street Bank and Trust under the terms of the grant award include: (1) a 1/3 FTE program coordinator selected from among the College's senior business faculty ($15,000); (2) a $3,000 stipend for the six (6) members of Stonehill's business faculty who will be assigned to organize the *Business Challenge* high school programs ($18,000); (3) secretarial support for the project ($5,000); and (4) honoraria (and related expenses) for business leaders and other guests invited to participate in *State Street Scholars* program offerings ($10,000). Stonehill College will assume all other costs associated with the program including: (1) faculty benefits (e.g., insurance, retirement -- $5,922); (2) project-related travel ($3,000); (3) office supplies and equipment at $5,000; and (4) expenses for an annual recognition dinner for the Scholars and their sponsors ($2,000). Thus, the projected annual budget for the *State Street Scholars in Business Program* is $63,922.

In addition to the direct project expenses noted above the College will ensure that each student named as a *State Street Scholar* will have sufficient financial assistance available to successfully complete the entire undergraduate course of study. Among the funding available to support these and other minority students enrolled at Stonehill is

141

$250,000 in College-sponsored student financial assistance. This sum in addition to Federal and State grants and loans, as well as private benefaction, will provide the level of funding required by the *State Street Scholars*.

An itemized budget for the project is provided as Attachment III.

For further information regarding the *State Street Scholars in Business* proposal, please contact Dr. George J. Hagerty, Director of Corporate, Foundation, and Government Relations or Professor William A. Burke of the College's Department of Business Administration. The mailing address for both Dr. Hagerty and Professor Burke is Stonehill College, 320 Washington Street, North Easton, Massachusetts 02357.

*   *   *   *   *

Stonehill College -- A Distinct Academic Community: Since its founding in 1948, Stonehill College has quietly and tenaciously pursued an ideal: **Liberal education in the Judeo-Christian tradition is a powerful force**. Affiliated with the priests and brothers of the Congregation of Holy Cross, Stonehill is an independent, church-affiliated undergraduate institution situated on 375 acres in North Easton, Massachusetts.

The College enrolls 1,950 full-time students in its Day Division; Stonehill serves an additional 1,000 students in its Evening Division program, many of whom have interrupted their schooling for family and financial reasons. The College offers degrees in three major concentrations: the liberal arts and related professional disciplines, the sciences and business administration.

Stonehill is a unique community, distinctly fashioned by faith, hard work, great expectations, and the resourceful planning and disciplined management essential to academic excellence. Over the course of the past decade, the College has strengthened its core curriculum, pioneered innovative international study options, supported faculty development programming and constructed essential facilities to serve better its core constituency: talented students -- many first-generation college students -- of modest means.

A Prospectus: The State Street Scholars In Business Program

Recently, Stonehill was recognized nationally as the only private college or university in Massachusetts to be selected for both **Barron's 300 Best Buys in College Education**, a guide to the colleges and universities that provide quality academic programs at cost-effective prices and Prentice Hall's **200 Most Selective Colleges: The Definitive Guide to America's First Choice Schools**.

Among the rich resources available to the community on the Stonehill College campus are: The Joseph W. Martin Jr. Institute for Law and Society, a Congressionally-mandated regional research and policy center; The W.B. Mason Forum on the Future of Southeastern Massachusetts; The Superintendent's Center for Educational Policy and Leadership; and the Horace Howard Senior Education Program, which provides tuition-free continuing education for senior citizens.

Attachment I
Stonehill College: A Community Profile
Accredited by The New England Association of Schools and Colleges

LOCATION: North Easton, Massachusetts
375 Acre Campus

FOUNDED: 1948

AFFILIATION: Holy Cross Fathers

ENROLLMENT: 1,954; Coeducational
75% Campus Residents

ACADEMIC PROGRAMS: **Bachelor of Arts (B.A.)**

American Studies	International Studies
College Studies (self-designed major)	Managerial Economics
	Mathematics
Communication	Modern Languages
Criminal Justice	Philosophy
Early Childhood Education	Political Science
Economics	Psychology
Elementary Education	Public Administration
English Studies	Religious Studies
Health Care Administration	Sociology
History	Secondary Education Certificate

Bachelor of Science in Business Administration (B.S.B.A.)

Accounting	Management

143

Finance   Marketing

Bachelor of Science (B.S.)

Biology   Computer Science
  (includes Med-Tech, Pre-   Math-Computer Science
  Dent, Pre-Med concentrations)   Medical Technology
Chemistry

SPECIAL ACADEMIC OPTIONS:
Study Abroad
Internships--Domestic/International
Exchange Program with 8 Area Colleges

FACULTY TO STUDENT RATIO:	17 to 1
AVERAGE CLASS SIZE:	23
COSTS: TUITION (AY 1993-94)	$11,230
ROOM & BOARD	$5,996

Attachment II
Duties of the Project Coordinator
and Program Faculty

Integral to the success of the *State Street Scholars in Business Program* will be the selection of seven (7) key staff members to oversee, coordinate, and implement the various program components. The roles of the Project Coordinator and Program Faculty (of six (6) members) are identified below:

Project Coordinator

The Project Coordinator will be a senior member of the College's business faculty and will be responsible for:

Serving as the liaison between the College, *State Street Bank, Business Challenge* high schools, and other appropriate institutions and organizations (e.g., Community Colleges, intern sites);

Serving as the liaison, internally between the *Program* and the various programs and constituencies within the College (e.g., other departments in the Academic Division, the Treasurer's office, the Registrar's office, the Counseling Center);

144

With the assistance of the Project Faculty and in consultation with *State Street Bank*, establishing and overseeing the administration of an annual management plan to ensure the successful achievement of all program objectives;

Supervising and evaluating all Project Faculty in their duties with respect to *Business Challenge, Explore*, and the *State Street Scholars* program components; and

Evaluating the program on an annual basis and submitting to the Community Affairs Division of *State Street Bank* the results of this evaluation (to be contained in the College's annual application for funding).

Program Faculty

The Program Faculty will be tenured or tenure-track members of the College's business department, department of economics, and/or department of computer science and will be responsible for:

Conducting on-site and campus-based activities with "paired schools" (based upon an annual action plan developed by the faculty member) -- please refer to pages 1 and 2 of the proposal;

Supervising the development of individualized business education plans for each advisee (*State Street Scholar*) assigned to the Program Faculty. (Each Program Faculty member will be assigned a minimum of one and maximum of three *Scholar* advisees.);

As assigned by the Project Coordinator, organizing and attending *State Street Scholar* seminars and other specialized program offerings (e.g., visitations to business sites and graduate schools, assisting in Career Services programming and the like); and

Teaching regular courses associated with the attainment of *Program* objectives.

State Street Scholars in Business Program

Proposed Budget
1993-1994

	SPONSOR COSTS	COLLEGE COSTS
I. A. PERSONNEL		
1.) Program Coordinator Part time ($15,000)	$15,000	
2.) Business Faculty 6 faculty members @ $3,000 ($18,000)	$18,000	
3.) Support Staff Part time secretary and support staff ($5,000)	$5,000	
TOTAL PERSONNEL (Salaries) ($38,000)	$38,000	
B. FRINGE BENEFITS (Professional staff only)		
1.) 21% of Personnel 7.65% FICA 10.00% Retirement 2.25% Medical 1.08% Life and Longterm Disability .005% Workman's Compensation		$5,922
TOTAL PERSONNEL ($43,922)	**$38,000**	**$5,922**
II. STUDENT SCHOLARSHIP Financial assistance awarded to program scholars		$250,000*
III. TRAVEL		
1.) Project-related Travel		$3,000

IV. SPECIAL EVENTS

    1.) Honoraria $10,000
        Expenses for 4 guest
        participants ($10,000)

    2.) Annual Recognition Dinner $2,000

V. MISCELLANEOUS

    1.) Office Supplies and Equipment $5,000

        TOTAL PROGRAM COSTS   **$48,000**   **$265,922**
        ($313,922)

* Figure reflects college-sponsored minority scholarship assistance available to minority students for the 1993-94 academic year.

Success Despite Foundation Restrictions:
Chicago Museum Weds Bricks & Mortar and Multiculturalism

The Institution: The Museum of Contemporary Art (MCA) was founded in 1967 to showcase temporary exhibitions of the best in international, national, and local contemporary art. The early years of the MCA saw a program of exhibitions that have become legendary in the art world, including Christo's wrapping of the MCA building in 1969. In 1979, the Education Department expanded its outreach programs for Chicago's schools and adult population. In the 1980's, the MCA embarked on an ambitious series of traveling exhibitions. In 1988, the MCA announced plans to build a new museum on the site of the Chicago Avenue Armory. The effort to fund, endow, and operate the new MCA is one of the most ambitious fundraising efforts in Chicago history. By March of 1993, over $45 million of the $55 million goal had been raised.

The Author: This proposal is a collaborative effort of Carolyn L. Stolper, chief development officer of the MCA, and Penelope Welz, of Staley/Robeson/Ryan/St. Lawrence. Ms. Stolper is responsible for having raised $45 million toward the campaign and runs all other fundraising programs. Previously, she was vice president for development and public affairs at AFS Intercultural Programs, Inc. an headed development departments at Playwrights Horizons and The National Theatre of the Deaf. She has a B.A. in Art History and a M.A. in Arts Administration from the University of Wisconsin and is the author of Successful Fundraising for Arts and Cultural Organizations (Oryx Press). Ms. Welz is an independent writer/producer specializing in print and electronic communications for non-profit organizations nationwide. In 1992, she received the Frank H. Robeson Memorial President's Award from Staley/Robeson/Ryan/St. Lawrence for outstanding work on behalf of the MCA.

Background: The following proposal to the Polk Bros. Foundation requests a grant of $1 million to establish an endowment for education as part of the Chicago Contemporary Campaign. In conversations subsequent to the proposal submission between the officials of the Foundation and the museum a specific plan was worked out to earmark their grant for an education endowment for multi-cultural students. The Polk Bros. Foundation only makes grants in the Chicago area and rarely awards grants for endowment. The Foundation made an exception to its limitation on endowments in this case because of the strength of the MCA's commitment to multi-cultural programming and a long-standing relationship.

August 28

Ms. Sandra P. Guthman
President
Polk Bros. Foundation
420 North Wabash Avenue, Suite 204
Chicago, Illinois 60611

Dear Sandy:

On behalf of the Museum of Contemporary Art, I am writing to request the Polk Bros. Foundation's consideration of a $1 million grant to the Chicago Contemporary Campaign to establish the Polk Bros. Foundation Educational Endowment Fund. A grant of this proportion will ensure the quality of the museum's outreach and education programs well into the next century.

The trustees and staff of the MCA are grateful for your consideration of this request and look forward to working with you to turn our dream of a new museum into a reality.

Sincerely,

Allen M. Turner
Chairman

A Proposal for

Polk Bros. Foundation

The Chicago Contemporary Campaign
Museum of Contemporary Art

"Once having marched over the margins of animal necessity, over the grim line of sheer subsistence, then man came to the deeper rituals of his bones, to the time for thinking things over -- to the dance, to the song, to the hours given to dreaming, once having so marched."

Carl Sandburg's words clearly articulate the artistic impulse found at the center of the human story. Throughout art we take joy in and struggle with expressing the wellspring of human experience. Art is the language by which we share and explore the most intimate and most profoundly moving aspects of the human spirit.

Contemporary art is the expression of this creative impulse at work today. Artists still seek to give voice and form to the human experience. Their work is filled with both the wonder and the grief of contemporary society. It has to do with justice and injustice, love and hate, war and peace. It struggles with all the issues, feelings and experiences that confront us and confound us. Contemporary art presents us with a new opportunity to explore what it means to be human and what it means to be alive in the 20th century.

The Museum of Contemporary Art (MCA) has been at the center of presenting the very best in the contemporary visual arts to metropolitan Chicago for 23 years. Since 1967, the MCA has invigorated this city and its citizens. Through its collection, exhibitions and educational programming, the MCA has remained at the cutting edge of contemporary art as it has sought to chronicle, understand and challenge contemporary society.

As it enters the new decade, the MCA has arrived at a pivotal juncture in its history. The museum has matured, in both program and stature, to a point where the physical constraints of its current facility have become critical. As these constraints now compromise the museum's ability to play a vital role in the cultural life of Chicago, the MCA trustees have chosen to address this problem through the construction of a new museum.

In May 1990, the State of Illinois formally transferred the Chicago Avenue Armory property, east of Michigan Avenue and the historic Water Tower, to the Museum of Contemporary Art for the construction of this new facility. The magnificent two-acre site will permit the creation of a world-class 125,000-square-foot building and sculpture garden of international significance. With triple the space of its current facility, the new museum will position the MCA to serve the cultural life of Chicago and to help ensure the preeminence of our city as a center for the arts well into the next century.

The Polk Bros. Foundation has already, through its leadership grant of $100,000, played an important role in the commencement of this effort. The Museum of Contemporary Art now seeks the continued assistance of the Polk

Bros. Foundation to bring this vision of a new museum into reality. Through a $1 million grant over four years, Polk Bros. Foundation can build on its prior gift to help ensure the new museum is representative of this city's rich artistic tradition and its dynamic future as a cultural center.

The new Museum Project

With the transfer of the Chicago Avenue Armory property to the MCA, numerous state, city, and community leaders have joined to endorse the project. Mayor Richard M. Daley, Honorary Chairman of the Chicago Contemporary Campaign said, ''Chicago has a reputation for great art and great architecture. This new building and sculpture garden will enhance that reputation. I am confident the citizens of Chicago will respond with enthusiasm to this new home for the Museum of Contemporary Art. I encourage all Chicagoans to invest in the cultural future of our city.'' In addition to its impact on the cultural community, the new museum will be a catalyst for arts-related economic development. The current museum and program have already been credited with helping to spawn the vibrant gallery business now found in Chicago's River North area.

Joining with other city and state leaders in voicing approval of the project, Governor Jim Edgar stated, ''The State's gift of the Chicago Avenue Armory Building to the MCA as the site for its new building was the beginning of what already promises to be one of the most exciting new building projects in the city in this century. We were delighted to be in this unique position to have such great impact on the future of the museum and the cultural vitality of Chicago.''

The museum will be free to take advantage of a variety of architectural options and to incorporate the latest technologies in both design and structure. The architectural plan calls for a 125,000-square-foot building centered on a landscaped sculpture garden. The combination of building and garden will create an internationally recognized cultural and architectural landmark.

While the museum's ability to contribute to Chicago's stature as a center for tourism and architecture and its ability to encourage the growing arts sector of the economy are important, these factors alone are not sufficient reason to embark on such a monumental project. The primary purpose of the new museum project is to provide an environment in which citizens of metropolitan Chicago and visitors to this region can fully engage in and reflect on the art and culture of their time.

To fulfill this purpose, the museum will offer extensive gallery space for traveling exhibitions, the permanent collection and large-scale exterior sculpture. The new facility will also support educational programming in classroom, studio, auditorium, and library space and encourage a vibrant institutional life through special event facilities, cafe and museum shop. Together, each of these components will work in concert to create an atmosphere which opens the transforming world of contemporary art to the broadest possible audience.

Exhibition Space

The museum's interior exhibition space will include gallery groupings of various sizes. The larger galleries will make it possible for the MCA to host and launch traveling exhibitions of major scale and importance. Currently, many such exhibitions do not come to Chicago because of gallery space limitations. The multiple-gallery design will also enable the museum to present simultaneous exhibitions and eliminate the need to close during installations.

In addition, expanded gallery options will create an appropriate space for the ongoing exhibition of the MCA's acclaimed permanent collection. One of Chicago's cultural treasures, the collection contains many masterpieces of the 20th century. When presented in tandem with other exhibits, the collection sets an invaluable context in which to appreciate and to understand more contemporary works. Enhanced facilities for the permanent collection will also make the MCA an attractive vessel for donated works from the world-renowned private collections found in and around Chicago. The foresight and judgement of this collecting community has brought some of the best contemporary art from across the globe to Chicago. A new museum will help ensure these masterpieces find a permanent home here rather than in another city.

One of the museum's most striking exhibition features will be the sculpture garden. The garden will occupy approximately one-half of the museum's two-acre site and will figure prominently in the architectural and aesthetic impact of the building. It will offer the proper setting to exhibit large-scale exterior works, either on loan or from the permanent collection. The garden will also serve as a catalyst for works through site-specific commissions and installations. It will also offer the general public a refreshing outdoor oasis in the midst of downtown.

Education Space

The MCA has long been recognized as one of the primary sources in metropolitan Chicago for information and educational programs on contemporary art. The museum presents regular exhibit tours, lectures and outreach programs to senior citizens and students at every level. These programs expose participants to the aesthetic aspects of contemporary art at the same time they explore related issues in psychology, sociology, technology, language arts, history, science and mathematics.

The new museum will provide classrooms and space capable of supporting an even larger education and outreach program. These rooms will be equipped with the latest audio and video technology. The education section will also include a school-group orientation room as well as wet and dry "studio" space to allow for experiential learning. The entire education program will be supported by an expanded library. The library will include an extensive collection of books, archive material from artists, slides, videotapes, photographs, recordings, and computerized storage and retrieval systems.

Support Facilities

The museum will be a gathering place and focal point of cultural and civic activities for the city. Its support facilities will be designed to accommodate a wide range of multi-disciplinary programs and events. Catering and meeting support services will be availabe through the building. In addition, specail areas will be designated for receptions, informal gatherings, and other social occasions. To augment these public spaces and services, a cafe and museum store will be included in the design. The cafe will overlook the lake and sculpture garden. The museum store will offer gifts, children's items and arts-related books.

A Plan to Achieve The Dream

The vision for the museum grew out of a comprehensive planning process which has encompassed all aspects of the museum's program and its constituencies. Directed by a trustee steering committee and senior management, the process has involved, and will continue to involve, trustees; staff; auxiliary boards; volunteer and membership groups; neighborhood organizations; city and state agencies; major individual, foundation, and corporate donors; and the general museum audience. In addition, professional counsel has been retained, on a selective basis, to provide technical advice on critical components of the plan outside the expertise of trustees or project staff.

The plan has four major components: leadership, fund-raising, facility design, and audience/membership development.

Leadership

The Museum of Contemporary Art has recently taken several significant steps to prepare its Board of Trustees and its senior management staff to take on the added responsibility of the museum project and to be more representative of the city. In December 1988, the Board adopted resolutions defining the roles and responsibilities of trustees, establishing guidelines for Board committee composition, and instituting terms of office with mandatory rotation to ensure Board rejuvenation. Recent additions to the Board include Edward F. Anixter, J. Paul Beitler, Marshall Front, Jack Guthman, Penny Prizker, Marjorie Susman, and former Gov. James R. Thompson. Allen M. Turner was elected Chairman of the Board in June 1991.

Concurrent with these Board chages, a position description was developed and adopted for the Chief Executive Officer and Director of the museum. The description clearly defined professional requirements in two key areas: institution building and artistic leadership. It also gave the Director a broader range of managment authority and accountability.

After an international search, the Board of Trustees hired Kevin E. Consey as the MCA's CEO and Director. Mr. Consey came to the MCA in November 1989 from Newport Harbor Art Museum where he served as Director for seven years. While in Newport, he gained valuable experience by launching a similar museum project.

The museum has also strengthened its management team by creating the position of Associate Director. The Associate Director, Mary E. Ittelson, is responsible for all operational aspects of the museum, short and long-range planning and implementation of the new museum project. Ms. Ittelson's presence adds important depth to the MCA's senior staff.

Fund-raising

Fund-raising plans for the museum call for a five-year $55 million campaign to endow and operate the museum. Given the complexity of a campaign of this magnitude, the museum retained the consulting firm of Staley/Robeson/Ryan/St. Lawrence, Inc. to conduct a feasibility/planning study and assist with campaign planning and implementation. The campaign feasibility/planning study, adopted by the MCA trustees in May 1989, found a favorable fund-raising climate for a project of this type and size.

In just a year, significant headway has been made in addressing each of the major recommendations outlined in the Staley/Robeson study: Carolyn L. Stolper, CFRE was appointed Chief Development Officer; a more vigorous and comprehensive annual development program has been initiated; the campaign planning program has been instituted; and the campaign effort was launched. Under the volunteer direction of Jerome H. Stone, Chicago Contemporary Campaign Chairman, the campaign's leadership gift phase has already generated more than $40 million in commitments from a select group of friends and trustees. This early success has confirmed the feasibility study's confidence in the MCA's ability to attract campaign gifts in sufficient numbers and amounts to reach the project's ambitious goal.

Facility Design

Trustees and staff have carefully researched trends in museum design and the architecture of public spaces to establish basic parameters for the museum. A preliminary building program document with detailed specification has been developed in conjunction with architectural counsel. This document includes general space requirements such as the relationship between galleries, education facilities and support spaces as well as the functional requirements of lighting, environmental controls and security.

Early grants from the Chicago Community Trust, The Joyce Foundation, the Illinois Arts Council, and the Polk Bros. Foundation has underwritten the development and implementation of the initial phases of planning. Marking another important step in implementing the museum plan, the architect selection process began in summer of 1990 with over 200 architects submitting nominations. A committee of trustees, art experts and architectural professional first narrowed the initial list ot twenty-three semi-finalists and then revealed the six finalists at a special program on January 28. At the public announcement of the Chicago Contemporary Campaign on May 21, Josef Paul Kleihues of Berlin was introduced as the architect selected to design the new building and sculpture garden for Chicago's Museum of Contemporary Art. The architect will work with the MCA to refine existing plans and develop a design by early 1992. The museum is slated for completion in the Spring of 1995.

Audience/Membership Development

The building of a cultural institution of this magnitude demands that serious consideration be given to the constituencies it will serve and to their ability to support the on-going life of the institution. The MCA has focused upon constituency assessment and development as a top priority from the beginning of this planning process for the new museum.

The first component in this effort was a market research project conducted by Leo Burnett and company on behalf of the MCA. Extensive data was gathered on the needs, wants, and perceptions of the museum's current and potential audiences. This information was then translated into an outreach program to increase public awareness and museum membership.

The outreach program began with the "What Will It Do To You?" campaign developed through <u>pro bono</u> services from Mitchner & Ross. The campaign, still underway, utilizes eye-catching images in print ads, direct mail pieces, street banners and bus cards to promote greater awareness of the museum and its services. To capitalize on the increased public awareness, a companion membership drive has been launched. These efforts resulted in a 60% increase in museum attendance during the first month.

The museum remains committed to reaching out to Chicago's many diverse communities. Through targeted audience awareness campaigns, and its highly praised school outreach program which serves 13,000 inner city school children, the MCA has developed an exemplary track record. The museum expects to continue to build on these successes and become a cultural destination for all of Chicago.

These outreach activities are just the first in a five-year process that runs concurrently with the building of the new museum. The expertise of an expanded development and membership staff combined with these programs will ensure that the museum rests on a broad constituent foundation representative of metropolitan Chicago's keen interest in and concern for the arts.

A Grant from Polk Bros. Foundation

The Museum of Contemporary Art respectfully requests that Polk Bros. Foundation express its continued leadership of the Chicago Contemporary Campaign by making a $1 million grant over four years to help bring metropolitan Chicago a new Museum of Contemporary Art. In recognition of this pace-setting contribution to the cultural future of Chicago, the Museum of Contemporary Art is prepared to permanently connect the name of Polk Bros. Foundation with an aspect of the facility worthy of this investment and the prominence of the Foundation.

Although the museum will be happy to discuss any naming opportunity the Foundation considers appropriate, the museum is suggesting that the Foundation designate a gift to establish an Education Endowment.

Polk Bros. Foundation
Educational Endowment Fund

One of the most exciting aspects of the new museum will be the opportunity to provide significantly enhanced educational programs for the general public and public school children. To ensure the quality of programs, several educational endowments have been created.

We hope the Foundation will consider a leadership gift of $1 million to be paid over four years, designated to the General Education Endowment Fund.

WINNING GRANT PROPOSALS

Our new emphasis on expanded educational programming will be made possible by a larger facility comprised of an orientation hall, teaching gallery and classrooms which will enable the museum to accommodate a growing audience of contemporary art enthusiasts as well as those not yet exposed to contemporary art. The latest in museum technology and instructional media will be used for education. Appreciation and understanding of contemporary art will be nurtured through lectures, films, symposia and classes.

A wide range of programs for the general public and public school students will address a broad audience, from children to senior citizens, including college and community groups. Strengthening of the museum's outreach programs will also help to attract and serve special audiences, including the underserved, and to stimulate interest among multi-cultural communities. The MCA's educational programming will be uniquely suited to enhance understanding of the significant issues of the day.

In light of the greatly-expanded potential audience for contemporary art in general, as well as the need to provide quality education for the many school children whose only exposure to contemporary art may be through the museum, the MCA plans to incorporate cross-cultural and intergenerational activities into its art education program as well as to introduce topical issues. Already, the museum's structured school and senior citizen outreach programs have brought contemporary art into the lives of thousands of students, teachers and seniors.

Exhibition-related education will be user-friendly and non-threatening, while encouraging exploration and questioning. It will take the form of printed gallery guides and catalogues prepared for all major exhibitions, as well as docent-led gallery talks, portable audio aids, lectures, orientation videos, and didactic wall signs. Interactive, hands-on activities for children will encourage them to become personally involved with the art on display.

Permanent Recognition

A $1 million Polk Bros. Foundation grant will be a pace-setting example to Chicago's philanthropic community regarding the importance of this endeavor and the kind of commitments required to bring this dream to fruition. Polk Bros. Foundation will forever be associated with a group of cultural leaders who have the foresight to give Chicago what will surely be one of its most acclaimed cultural centers and architectural landmarks.

We appreciate your consideration of this important step on behalf of Chicago's cultural future.

Gordon Jay Frost is Vice President of Philanthropic Resources International Management Associates (PRIMA), a private consulting firm which serves to link non-profit organizations and international corporations. He has previously served in the development office of Meridian International Center, the Washington office of The American Film Institute and the Literature and Inter-Arts Programs of the National Endowment for the Arts. Mr. Frost is a member of the Board of Directors of the American Prospect Research Association (APRA), a 1,400-member national organization of researchers in development, and past-President of the APRA-Metro D.C. Chapter. He has been featured as a speaker at conferences of the APRA and the National Society of Fund Raising Executives.

In 1990, Mr. Frost received the American Prospect Research Association's first Award for Excellence in Prospect Research for his essay, *The Route to the Golden Temple: Identifying Japanese Corporate Prospects in the Era of Good Corporate Citizenship*, which was included in The Taft Group's collection, *The American Prospector*. In 1991, The Taft Group released Frost's *Japanese Resources: A Guide to Information on Japanese Business and Grantmaking Activities*. During the same year, he co-authored a paper on *Washington Think-Tanks: An Information Channel* as part of the American delegation to the Third International Conference on Japanese Information in Science, Technology and Commerce in 1991.

A graduate of the Interlochen Arts Academy and the University of Michigan, Mr. Frost now lives and works in Washington, D.C.